Table Of Contents

Part 7: Troubleshooting and Optimization

Part 8: Real-World Case Studies

Part 9: Future-Proofing Your Jira Setup

Appendices

- Appendix A: Jira Query Language (JQL) Cheat Sheet
- Appendix B: Keyboard Shortcuts for Power Users
- Appendix C: Glossary of Jira Terms for Developers
- Appendix D: Resources and Tools for Further Learning

~ Conclusion

Disclaimer

This book is an independent resource and is not officially affiliated with, endorsed by, or sponsored by any company, organization, or trademark holder referenced within. All trademarks, service marks, product names, and company names or logos mentioned are the property of their respective owners. Use of these names or terms is solely for identification and reference purposes, and no association or endorsement by the respective trademark holder is implied. The content of this book is based on publicly available information, the author's research, and personal insights. This book is intended for educational and informational purposes only.

Welcome & What You'll Learn

Welcome to *Jira for Developers: Streamlining Your Development Projects*

Jira has become the go-to tool for development teams looking to organize their work, enhance collaboration, and streamline software delivery. Whether you are an individual developer, part of a growing startup, or embedded in an enterprise-scale team, mastering Jira can significantly boost your productivity and efficiency.

This book is designed to help developers tailor Jira to their specific needs, enabling them to move beyond basic issue tracking and harness the full power of this platform. Unlike general Jira guides, this book focuses on the developer's perspective—how to optimize Jira for coding workflows, integrate it seamlessly with your existing toolchain, and automate repetitive tasks to minimize friction.

By the time you finish this book, you'll have a deep understanding of how Jira can become more than just a ticketing system—it can be a central hub for your entire development cycle, from planning to deployment.

Why This Book?

Many Jira guides focus on project managers or agile coaches, leaving developers to figure out the technical aspects on their own. This book is different. It speaks directly to developers, offering hands-on guidance for setting up, configuring, and using Jira effectively in a software development context.

We cover:

- How to configure Jira for your development workflows
- Best practices for managing sprints, backlogs, and epics
- Seamless integration with version control systems like GitHub, GitLab, and Bitbucket
- Automating manual processes with Jira Automation and APIs
- Debugging common configuration issues
- Optimizing Jira for performance in large-scale projects
- Case studies from real-world development teams

Whether you're new to Jira or looking to refine your existing workflows, this book will provide actionable insights that help you become a more efficient and organized developer.

What You'll Learn

Here's a glimpse of what you can expect from this book:

1. Introduction to Jira

- Understand Jira's role in modern software development.
- Learn why Jira is essential for developers and not just project managers.

2. Setting Up Jira for Development Teams

- Explore the differences between Jira Cloud and Server deployments.
- Learn how to install, configure, and set up Jira for software teams.
- Assign roles and permissions effectively to maintain workflow integrity.

3. Configuring Jira for Efficiency

- Customize issue types and workflows for development projects.

- Set up agile-friendly boards (Scrum and Kanban) to optimize team productivity.
- Automate repetitive tasks to streamline your development cycle.

4. Advanced Workflow Management

- Master backlog prioritization and sprint planning techniques.
- Integrate Jira with code review tools to enhance development speed.
- Learn how to handle bugs, dependencies, and technical debt within Jira.

5. Integrations and Extensions

- Connect Jira with CI/CD pipelines for seamless deployments.
- Integrate Jira with version control platforms to track changes efficiently.
- Extend Jira's functionality with marketplace apps and custom scripts.

6. Best Practices for Developers

- Improve sprint estimations and backlog management.
- Balance technical debt with feature development.
- Enhance collaboration in remote development environments.

7. Troubleshooting and Optimization

- Debug common Jira configuration issues.
- Optimize Jira for performance in large-scale projects.
- Learn security best practices to protect sensitive development data.

8. Real-World Case Studies

- Explore real-world examples of teams using Jira to optimize their workflows.
- Learn from successful DevOps and agile transformations.

9. Future-Proofing Your Jira Setup

- Discover how AI-driven development is shaping the future of Jira.
- Stay ahead of cloud-first trends and prepare your workflows accordingly.

How to Use This Book

This book is structured to be both a step-by-step guide and a reference manual. You can follow it sequentially to build your Jira expertise from the ground up or jump directly to the chapters most relevant to your needs.

Each chapter includes:

- **Hands-on tutorials** to guide you through Jira setup and configuration.
- **Best practices** from industry experts to help you avoid common pitfalls.
- **Pro tips** to improve your efficiency with Jira's advanced features.
- **Case studies** to see how real teams solve development challenges with Jira.

By the end of this book, you'll have the knowledge and confidence to configure Jira in a way that best suits your development workflows. You'll move beyond the basics and turn Jira into a powerful ally in your software development journey.

Let's get started!

Part 1:
Introduction to Jira

What Is Jira and Why Developers Need It

Jira is a powerful tool for managing software development projects, enabling teams to track issues, manage workflows, and collaborate effectively. Originally created by Atlassian as a bug-tracking system, Jira has evolved into a comprehensive platform that supports agile development, DevOps workflows, and complex project management needs.

At its core, Jira allows development teams to:

- **Track and prioritize work** using issues, epics, and sprints.
- **Define custom workflows** to match their software development lifecycle.
- **Integrate with development tools** such as GitHub, Bitbucket, and Jenkins.
- **Automate tasks and reporting** to enhance efficiency.

Jira's flexibility makes it useful for everything from managing simple task lists to orchestrating enterprise-scale software projects. It supports agile methodologies like Scrum and Kanban while also being adaptable to hybrid or custom workflows.

The Different Flavors of Jira

Atlassian offers several versions of Jira, each tailored to different use cases:

- **Jira Software** – The most commonly used version for development teams, supporting Scrum, Kanban, roadmaps, and DevOps integrations.
- **Jira Work Management** – Designed for non-technical teams to manage projects and tasks without the complexity of software development workflows.
- **Jira Service Management** – Focuses on IT service management (ITSM), incident resolution, and help desk operations.
- **Jira Align** – A higher-level planning tool for scaling agile practices across large organizations.

For developers, *Jira Software* is the primary focus, as it offers the tools needed to manage code, track bugs, and coordinate releases efficiently.

Why Developers Need Jira

Many developers view project management tools as overhead—something that adds extra work rather than making their lives easier. However, Jira, when used correctly, can significantly improve a developer's workflow, reducing friction and increasing productivity.

Here's why developers should embrace Jira:

1. Centralized Issue Tracking

Jira provides a single source of truth for tracking tasks, bugs, feature requests, and technical debt. Instead of managing work through emails, chat messages, or spreadsheets, developers can use Jira's issue tracking to stay organized.

- Assign issues to team members.
- Set priorities based on impact and urgency.
- Link issues to code changes for better traceability.

2. Seamless Integration with Development Tools

Jira integrates with the most commonly used development tools, making it easy to sync work across the software lifecycle:

- **Version Control Systems** – Link Jira issues to commits, branches, and pull requests in GitHub, GitLab, or Bitbucket.
- **CI/CD Pipelines** – Automate deployments with tools like Jenkins, GitHub Actions, and CircleCI.
- **IDEs and Command-Line Tools** – Work with Jira directly from JetBrains IDEs (IntelliJ IDEA, WebStorm) or through CLI tools.

3. Agile and DevOps Support

Jira is built with agile teams in mind, offering robust features for:

- **Sprint planning** – Organize work into sprints with clear goals and deadlines.
- **Kanban boards** – Visualize and optimize workflow using drag-and-drop tasks.
- **Backlog management** – Prioritize features and technical debt in a structured way.
- **DevOps metrics** – Track cycle time, deployment frequency, and other key performance indicators.

4. Custom Workflows for Development Teams

Every development team has unique workflows. Jira's workflow customization allows teams to define:

- **Issue lifecycles** (e.g., "To Do → In Progress → Code Review → Testing → Done").
- **Custom statuses** for better clarity (e.g., "Blocked," "Awaiting QA").
- **Automations** to reduce manual work (e.g., auto-assigning issues based on labels or triggers).

5. Better Collaboration and Visibility

Jira enables transparency in development projects:

- Product managers can see what's being worked on without disrupting developers.
- QA testers can track bug fixes and regression testing cycles.
- Developers can communicate progress through comments, mentions, and linked issues.

With built-in notifications, mentions, and integrations with Slack, Confluence, and Microsoft Teams, Jira ensures that developers and stakeholders stay aligned without excessive meetings.

Overcoming Common Developer Frustrations with Jira

Some developers resist using Jira due to perceived complexity or unnecessary bureaucracy. Here's how to mitigate common concerns:

Developer Concern	Solution

Too many fields and statuses	Customize issue screens to show only relevant fields.
Manual updates feel like extra work	Use Jira Automation to update statuses and assignments dynamically.
Jira is slow and bloated	Optimize performance by using filters, dashboards, and Jira Query Language (JQL).
Difficult to find relevant issues	Use saved searches, issue links, and dashboards for better navigation.
Too many notifications	Adjust notification preferences to avoid unnecessary Jira spam.

By fine-tuning Jira to suit developers' workflows, teams can eliminate unnecessary complexity and maximize its value.

When Should Developers Start Using Jira?

The earlier a development team adopts Jira, the better it can structure its workflows. Here are key moments when Jira becomes essential:

- **In small teams** – Even in a startup, Jira helps structure work without relying on unorganized task lists.
- **When projects scale** – As a project grows, Jira's ability to track dependencies and priorities becomes invaluable.
- **During agile adoption** – Scrum and Kanban workflows become easier to manage with Jira's built-in tools.
- **When collaborating across teams** – Jira bridges the gap between developers, QA, product managers, and operations.

Final Thoughts

Jira is more than just a project management tool—it's a powerful platform that, when configured correctly, can enhance the productivity of any development team. By embracing Jira, developers can reduce overhead, improve collaboration, and streamline their workflow from coding to deployment.

In the next chapter, we'll explore **Jira's role in modern software development**, diving deeper into how it aligns with agile, DevOps, and continuous delivery practices.

Jira's Role in Modern Software Development

Software development has evolved significantly over the past few decades. From traditional waterfall methodologies to agile and DevOps-driven workflows, teams now require tools that offer flexibility, transparency, and efficiency. Jira has emerged as a key platform that supports these modern development practices, helping teams manage everything from sprint planning to issue tracking and continuous integration.

With distributed teams, rapid release cycles, and the increasing complexity of software products, developers need a tool that not only organizes their work but also integrates seamlessly with their existing development ecosystem. Jira meets these demands by providing structured workflows, automation, and deep integration with development tools.

How Jira Supports Modern Development Methodologies

Jira is designed to align with the most commonly used software development methodologies, ensuring teams can manage their projects effectively while keeping development streamlined.

1. Agile Software Development

Agile methodologies, particularly Scrum and Kanban, have become the dominant frameworks for modern software teams. Jira is built with agile teams in mind, offering features that facilitate:

- **Sprint Planning** – Developers can define and prioritize work for each sprint.
- **Backlog Management** – Teams can manage product backlogs efficiently and break work into epics and user stories.
- **Work Visibility** – Jira's Scrum and Kanban boards provide a clear visual representation of progress.
- **Sprint Retrospectives** – Teams can analyze sprint performance using Jira reports such as burndown charts and velocity tracking.

For teams practicing Scrum, Jira provides sprint and backlog management tools, while Kanban teams benefit from customizable boards that allow real-time tracking of work in progress.

2. DevOps and Continuous Integration/Continuous Deployment (CI/CD)

Modern software development relies on DevOps practices to ensure fast, reliable software delivery. Jira plays a crucial role in DevOps by:

- **Tracking development work** – Developers can link Jira issues to commits, branches, and pull requests in GitHub, GitLab, and Bitbucket.
- **Automating deployments** – Jira integrates with CI/CD tools such as Jenkins, GitHub Actions, and CircleCI, triggering builds and deployments directly from Jira tickets.
- **Incident Management** – When issues arise in production, Jira can be used to track incidents, assign fixes, and document resolution steps.

By integrating Jira with DevOps pipelines, development teams can automate repetitive tasks and ensure that software changes are traceable from planning to production.

3. Managing Technical Debt and Code Quality

Technical debt is an inevitable part of software development, but managing it effectively ensures long-term maintainability. Jira helps teams:

- **Track technical debt** by tagging and categorizing issues related to refactoring or outdated code.
- **Prioritize bug fixes** alongside new feature development to maintain a healthy codebase.
- **Integrate with code review tools** to ensure high-quality pull requests and enforce coding standards.

Using Jira's reporting and automation features, teams can ensure technical debt does not accumulate unchecked, maintaining long-term development velocity.

4. Cross-Team Collaboration

Modern software development is rarely confined to a single team. Developers, QA testers, product managers, and operations teams all work together to deliver products. Jira facilitates this collaboration by:

- **Providing shared boards and dashboards** that give all stakeholders visibility into progress.
- **Integrating with communication tools** like Slack, Microsoft Teams, and Confluence.
- **Allowing automated notifications and mentions** to keep team members informed without excessive meetings.

By acting as a centralized hub for all development-related discussions and tracking, Jira reduces miscommunication and enhances team efficiency.

Key Benefits of Using Jira in Software Development

Jira is more than just a task management tool; it is a comprehensive development management platform. Here's how it benefits modern software teams:

Benefit	How It Helps Developers
Improved Work Visibility	Developers can see exactly what needs to be worked on and track progress easily.
Seamless Integration with Dev Tools	Connects with Git repositories, CI/CD pipelines, and monitoring tools.
Customizable Workflows	Teams can define their own development processes instead of using rigid structures.
Automation of Repetitive Tasks	Jira Automation eliminates the need for manual updates and assignments.
Data-Driven Decision Making	Reports and analytics provide insights into development velocity and bottlenecks.
Scalability	Works for small teams and large enterprises, adapting to different workflows.

When to Introduce Jira in a Development Workflow

For development teams that are not yet using Jira, it's best to introduce it at key milestones:

- **Early-stage startups** – Implement Jira when work begins to scale beyond a simple to-do list.

- **Growing teams** – When multiple developers work together, Jira helps maintain organization and prevents work duplication.
- **Enterprise projects** – For large-scale development efforts, Jira ensures structured project tracking and cross-team coordination.
- **Transitioning to Agile or DevOps** – Teams adopting agile or DevOps practices benefit greatly from Jira's built-in features.

Conclusion

Jira plays a vital role in modern software development by supporting agile methodologies, integrating with development pipelines, and improving collaboration. By leveraging Jira's powerful features, developers can spend more time writing code and less time on administrative overhead.

Part 2:
Setting Up Jira for Development Teams

Choosing the Right Jira Deployment: Cloud vs. Server

Before diving into Jira's setup and configuration, it's essential to choose the right deployment option for your development team. Atlassian offers two primary hosting options for Jira Software:

- **Jira Cloud** – Hosted and managed by Atlassian, providing ease of use and automatic updates.
- **Jira Data Center (Self-Hosted)** – Installed and managed by your team, offering greater control and customization.

Each option has its own advantages and trade-offs, depending on your team's size, security requirements, customization needs, and budget. In this chapter, we'll explore the key differences between **Jira Cloud** and **Jira Data Center (previously Jira Server)** to help you determine which best fits your development workflow.

Understanding Jira Cloud

What Is Jira Cloud?

Jira Cloud is a **fully managed, web-based version of Jira** that Atlassian hosts on its infrastructure. It is the easiest way to get started with Jira without worrying about setup, maintenance, or system administration.

Key Benefits of Jira Cloud

- **No Installation or Maintenance** – Atlassian handles all software updates, security patches, and server management.
- **Automatic Updates & New Features** – Cloud users get the latest Jira features as soon as they are released.
- **Scalability** – Atlassian manages the infrastructure, making it easy to scale Jira as your team grows.
- **Built-in Integrations** – Seamless connectivity with other Atlassian cloud products like Confluence, Bitbucket, and Trello.
- **Security & Compliance** – Atlassian provides data encryption, compliance certifications (SOC 2, ISO 27001), and backup management.

Limitations of Jira Cloud

- **Limited Customization** – While Jira Cloud allows for custom workflows and automations, it has fewer deep configuration options than the self-hosted version.
- **Performance Constraints** – For large-scale enterprises with thousands of users, performance tuning options are limited compared to self-hosted deployments.
- **Data Residency Concerns** – Data is stored on Atlassian's servers, which may be a concern for organizations with strict data residency requirements.

- **Dependency on Atlassian's Uptime** – Any downtime on Atlassian's side impacts all cloud users, though their uptime is generally high.

Best for…

- **Startups and small teams** who need a quick and hassle-free setup.
- **Teams that prioritize ease of use and automatic updates** over deep customizations.
- **Businesses that already use other Atlassian cloud products** like Bitbucket, Trello, or Confluence.
- **Companies that don't want to manage infrastructure, security, or backups manually.**

Understanding Jira Data Center (Self-Hosted)

What Is Jira Data Center?

Jira Data Center is **a self-hosted version of Jira** that runs on your own servers or private cloud infrastructure. It is ideal for teams that need complete control over their Jira environment, including data security, advanced customization, and performance tuning.

Note: Atlassian officially **discontinued Jira Server licenses in February 2021**, meaning that new self-hosted deployments must use **Jira Data Center**, which offers high availability and scalability features.

Key Benefits of Jira Data Center

- **Full Control Over Hosting** – Your team manages the infrastructure, allowing for deeper customization and security configurations.
- **Enhanced Performance** – Self-hosted Jira can be fine-tuned to handle large-scale projects, making it ideal for enterprise teams.
- **Data Security & Compliance** – Organizations with strict security policies or data residency requirements can host Jira in a private data center.
- **Custom Plugins & Integrations** – Unlike Jira Cloud, which limits certain third-party add-ons, self-hosted Jira allows full access to custom plugins and API modifications.
- **No Forced Updates** – Your team decides when to apply updates, preventing unexpected changes that might impact workflows.

Limitations of Jira Data Center

- **Complex Setup & Maintenance** – Requires an internal IT team to manage installation, performance tuning, backups, and security patches.
- **Higher Cost** – Jira Data Center requires a larger upfront investment in hardware and infrastructure.
- **Slower Access to New Features** – Unlike Jira Cloud, which gets frequent automatic updates, self-hosted Jira updates require manual upgrades.
- **Ongoing Administration Required** – Managing user roles, permissions, and system maintenance requires dedicated effort.

Best for…

- **Enterprises and large-scale development teams** that need high-performance issue tracking.
- **Organizations with strict data security requirements** that need to store Jira data on-premises.
- **Teams that require extensive customizations** beyond what Jira Cloud allows.
- **Companies with dedicated IT resources** to manage server infrastructure, updates, and maintenance.

Jira Cloud vs. Jira Data Center: A Side-by-Side Comparison

Feature	Jira Cloud	Jira Data Center (Self-Hosted)
Hosting	Managed by Atlassian	Hosted on your own infrastructure
Setup & Maintenance	No setup required, instant access	Requires IT team for setup and ongoing management
Scalability	Scales automatically	Requires server upgrades and load balancing
Performance	Optimized for most use cases, but with some limits	Fully tunable for high-performance needs
Customization	Limited deep customizations	Full control over configurations and custom add-ons
Security & Compliance	Security handled by Atlassian, meets industry standards	Full control over security measures, good for strict compliance requirements
Plugin Support	Limited Marketplace apps available	Full access to custom plugins and private integrations
Software Updates	Frequent automatic updates	Manual updates required (scheduled by IT team)
Cost	Subscription-based pricing (lower initial cost)	Higher upfront infrastructure cost, but fixed licensing fees
Best For	Small to mid-sized teams, agile startups, businesses preferring managed solutions	Large enterprises, teams requiring high customization and security, companies with IT infrastructure

Making the Right Choice for Your Team

Selecting the right Jira deployment depends on your team's priorities. Here's a quick decision guide:

Choose Jira Cloud If:

■ You want a **hassle-free, managed solution** with minimal IT overhead.
■ Your team values **instant access to updates and new features** without manual upgrades.
■ You need **fast setup and easy scalability** without server management.
■ Your company follows **standard security and compliance regulations** that Jira Cloud already meets.

Choose Jira Data Center (Self-Hosted) If:

■ You need **complete control** over data storage, security, and compliance.
■ Your team requires **extensive custom workflows, plugins, and integrations** beyond Jira Cloud's capabilities.
■ Your organization prefers **predictable performance** and wants to manage infrastructure internally.
■ Your team is **large-scale (hundreds or thousands of developers)** and needs fine-tuned Jira performance.

Conclusion

Choosing between **Jira Cloud and Jira Data Center** is a critical decision that impacts your development workflows, security policies, and overall efficiency.

- **Jira Cloud** is ideal for teams looking for **ease of use, quick deployment, and automatic updates** without infrastructure management.
- **Jira Data Center** is the right choice for **large enterprises, security-conscious teams, and those requiring deep customization** and control.

Once you've chosen the right deployment, the next step is **installing and configuring Jira for development workflows**, which we will cover in the next chapter.

Installing and Configuring Jira for Development Workflows

Once you have decided on the right Jira deployment for your development team—whether Jira Cloud or Jira Data Center (self-hosted)—the next step is **installation and initial configuration**. Proper setup ensures that your team can work efficiently, integrate development tools seamlessly, and avoid unnecessary administrative overhead.

This chapter provides a step-by-step guide for installing Jira (for self-hosted deployments) and configuring it for **development workflows**, covering key settings, best practices, and optimizations.

Installing Jira (For Self-Hosted Deployments)

Note: If you're using **Jira Cloud**, you can skip the installation process since Atlassian manages it for you. Simply sign up at [Atlassian's website] (https://www.atlassian.com/software/jira) and proceed to configuration.

System Requirements

Before installing Jira, ensure your system meets the following requirements (for Jira Data Center):

Minimum Requirements for Jira Data Center

Component	Recommended Specification
Operating System	Linux (Ubuntu, CentOS) or Windows Server
Java Version	Java 8+ (OpenJDK or Oracle JDK)
Database	PostgreSQL, MySQL, Microsoft SQL Server, Oracle DB
CPU	4+ Cores (for small teams)
Memory	8GB RAM (minimum), 16GB+ (for larger teams)
Disk Space	10GB+ (depends on project data)

Installation Steps for Jira Data Center

1. Download and Install Jira

- Go to the [Atlassian Download Center] (https://www.atlassian.com/software/jira/download).
- Select **Jira Software Data Center** and download the installation package.
- Run the installer for your operating system (Windows/Linux).

2. Database Configuration

- Choose **"I want to use an external database"** for better performance.
- Connect Jira to a **PostgreSQL, MySQL, or SQL Server** database.
- Run Jira's database setup wizard to complete the connection.

3. Set Up Application Properties

- Configure **base URL** (e.g., `https://jira.yourcompany.com`).
- Set up **admin credentials** and project keys.
- Enable **email notifications** for team collaboration.

4. Start Jira and Verify Installation

- Open Jira in your browser (`http://localhost:8080`).
- Log in with the **admin account** created during setup.
- Ensure that all **services and integrations** work properly.

Configuring Jira for Development Workflows

Once Jira is installed (or after signing up for Jira Cloud), it's time to configure it for software development. Below are key settings and best practices for development teams.

1. Creating a New Jira Project

Jira organizes tasks into **projects**, which serve as containers for development work.

Steps to Create a Project

1. **Go to Jira Dashboard → Projects → Create Project**
2. Choose a **project template** based on your workflow:
    - **Scrum** (for iterative sprints)
    - **Kanban** (for continuous delivery)
    - **Basic Software Project** (for general tracking)
3. Set a **project name and key** (e.g., "DEV" for a development project).
4. Assign project **lead and permissions** to team members.

Best Practice: Use a **consistent naming convention** (e.g., `BACKEND-123`, `MOBILE-456`) to make it easier to track issues across multiple teams.

---

2. Defining Issue Types for Development Workflows

Jira uses **issue types** to categorize tasks. The default types include:

Issue Type	Purpose
Story	A new feature or functionality
Task	General development work
Bug	A defect or problem in the code
Epic	A high-level collection of related stories
Subtask	A smaller part of a story or task

Customization Tip: You can create custom issue types like **Tech Debt**, **Code Review**, or **Spike (Research Task)** to better match your workflow.

---

3. Setting Up Agile Workflows

Customizing Jira Workflows for Developers

Jira workflows define how an issue progresses from **To Do** → **In Progress** → **Done**.

A typical **development workflow** might include:

- **To Do** → Work is planned but not started.
- **In Progress** → Development is active.
- **Code Review** → A developer has submitted a pull request.
- **QA Testing** → The feature is being tested by QA.
- **Done** → The issue is closed after deployment.

Best Practice: Add **automations** to update issue status automatically when a developer merges a pull request (e.g., moving an issue from "Code Review" to "Done").

---

4. Configuring Permissions for Developer Teams

Jira uses **permission schemes** to control access. A good setup for development teams might include:

Role	Permissions
Developers	Create, edit, and transition issues; log work
QA/Testers	Assign and reopen issues; add test results
Project Managers	Prioritize backlog, set sprint goals
Admins	Modify workflows, manage permissions

Best Practice: Use **Role-Based Access Control (RBAC)** instead of granting permissions manually for each user.

---

5. Integrating Jira with Development Tools

To streamline the development process, integrate Jira with:

- **GitHub, GitLab, or Bitbucket** – Link Jira issues to commits, branches, and pull requests.
- **CI/CD Tools (Jenkins, GitHub Actions)** – Automate builds and deployments from Jira.
- **Slack or Microsoft Teams** – Get notifications when issues are updated.
- **Confluence** – Document requirements and link them to Jira issues.

Best Practice: Use **Jira Automation** to automatically update issue statuses when a commit references an issue.

---

6. Automating Repetitive Tasks in Jira

Jira Automation allows teams to reduce manual work.

Examples of Useful Automations

- Move an issue to "Code Review" when a pull request is opened.
- Close an issue automatically when a feature is merged to `main`.
- Notify developers in Slack when a critical bug is assigned.

Best Practice: Use Jira's **If-This-Then-That** (IFTTT) automation rules to reduce administrative overhead.

---

7. Optimizing Jira Performance for Development Teams

If using Jira Data Center, performance tuning is crucial.

Optimization Tips

- **Use indexing** to speed up Jira searches.
- **Archive old projects** to reduce database load.
- **Enable caching** for faster issue retrieval.
- **Monitor system logs** for performance bottlenecks.

For Jira Cloud, Atlassian manages performance, but users can improve speed by **reducing unnecessary custom fields and workflows**.

Conclusion

Installing and configuring Jira correctly is the foundation for a streamlined development workflow. Whether using **Jira Cloud for simplicity** or **Jira Data Center for control**, teams must:

- ✔ **Choose the right project template** for their workflow.
- ✔ **Define issue types and statuses** to match development processes.
- ✔ **Set up permissions and integrations** for seamless collaboration.
- ✔ **Automate workflows** to reduce manual effort.

In the next chapter, we'll walk through **creating your first project** in Jira, covering **best practices for structuring issues, backlogs, and sprint planning**.

Creating Your First Project: Templates and Best Practices

Once Jira is installed and configured, the next step is to **create your first project**. Jira organizes work using **projects**, which act as containers for tracking issues, managing sprints, and coordinating development tasks.

Choosing the right **project template** is crucial for aligning Jira with your team's workflow. In this chapter, we'll cover:

- **Jira's project types and templates**
- **How to create a new project** in Jira Cloud and Jira Data Center
- **Best practices for setting up projects** for development teams

By the end of this chapter, you'll have a fully configured project ready for development.

Understanding Jira Project Types

When creating a new project, Jira offers different project types tailored to specific workflows.

1. Company-Managed vs. Team-Managed Projects

Jira Cloud provides two types of projects:

Project Type	Description	Best For
Company-Managed (Classic)	Full control over workflows, issue types, and permissions	Large teams, structured workflows
Team-Managed (Next-Gen)	Simplified setup with fewer admin controls	Small teams, quick setup

For development teams that require **custom workflows, integrations, and role-based permissions**, **Company-Managed Projects** are recommended.

2. Software, Business, and Service Projects

Jira provides different **project categories** based on team needs:

Project Category	Purpose	Best For
Software	Agile development (Scrum, Kanban, DevOps)	Development teams
Business	General task management (HR, marketing)	Non-technical teams
Service	IT service management (help desk, support)	IT and support teams

For developers, **Jira Software** projects are the ideal choice.

Selecting the Right Project Template

Jira Software offers **three main project templates** for development teams:

Template	Best Use Case	When to Choose
Scrum	Sprint-based development	If your team works in **iterations (sprints)**
Kanban	Continuous delivery	If your team uses a **flow-based system**
Bug Tracking	Issue tracking	If your team mainly tracks bugs and defects

Scrum vs. Kanban: Which Should You Choose?

Factor	Scrum	Kanban
Workflow	Sprint-based	Continuous flow
Best For	Teams that plan work in 1-4 week sprints	Teams with continuous, unplanned work
Sprint Planning	Yes	No
Backlog Management	Yes	No (optional)
Ideal For	Feature development	DevOps, bug tracking

Recommendation: If your team follows **Agile or Scrum**, choose the **Scrum template**. If your team focuses on **continuous releases or bug fixes**, **Kanban** is a better fit.

Creating a New Project in Jira

Steps to Create a New Project (Jira Cloud & Jira Data Center)

1. **Go to Jira Dashboard** → **Click "Projects"** → **"Create Project"**
2. **Select "Software Development"** as the project category
3. **Choose a template** (Scrum, Kanban, or Bug Tracking)
4. **Name the project and set a project key** (e.g., DEV for a development team)
5. **Choose project permissions**
   - Open: Anyone can access
   - Private: Only invited users
   - Limited: Only specific team members
6. **Click "Create"** to finalize the setup

Best Practices for Setting Up Development Projects

Once your project is created, follow these best practices for optimal workflow management.

1. Define Clear Issue Types

Ensure your project includes the necessary **issue types** for development:

Issue Type	Purpose
Epic	Large features or initiatives
Story	A user-focused feature request
Task	General development work
Bug	Fixing software defects
Subtask	A smaller piece of a task

Customization Tip: If your team frequently works on technical debt or research tasks, create custom issue types like **"Tech Debt"** or **"Spike"**.

2. Set Up a Meaningful Workflow

By default, Jira provides a simple **To Do → In Progress → Done** workflow. However, development teams often require more detailed workflows:

Status	Description
Backlog	Work planned for future sprints
To Do	Tasks ready for development
In Progress	Actively being worked on
Code Review	A pull request has been submitted
QA Testing	The feature is in testing
Done	The task is complete

Best Practice: Automate transitions, such as moving issues to **"Code Review"** when a pull request is created.

3. Configure Permissions & Roles

Assign appropriate permissions to team members based on their roles:

Role	Permissions
Developer	Create, update, and transition issues
QA Tester	Assign and reopen issues, add test results
Project Manager	Prioritize backlog, set sprint goals
Admin	Modify workflows, manage permissions

Tip: Use **Jira Groups** (e.g., dev-team, qa-team) to manage permissions efficiently.

4. Integrate with Development Tools

To enhance efficiency, integrate Jira with:

- **GitHub/GitLab/Bitbucket** – Automatically link commits and pull requests to Jira issues.
- **Jenkins/GitHub Actions** – Trigger builds and deployments from Jira.
- **Slack/Microsoft Teams** – Get real-time updates on issue changes.
- **Confluence** – Store development documentation linked to Jira issues.

Automation Tip: Use **Jira Automation** to transition issues when pull requests are merged.

5. Set Up Dashboards & Reports

Jira provides customizable **dashboards** to monitor development progress.

Recommended Dashboards for Development Teams

- **Sprint Progress** – Track active sprint progress.
- **Bug Status** – Monitor open, in-progress, and resolved bugs.
- **Code Review Queue** – View issues awaiting review.
- **Velocity Chart** – Measure how much work is completed per sprint.

Best Practice: Create a **team-wide dashboard** with key metrics to improve visibility.

Conclusion

Setting up your first Jira project correctly ensures **smooth development workflows** and **efficient issue tracking**.

✔ **Choose the right project type and template** (Scrum, Kanban, or Bug Tracking).
✔ **Define essential issue types** (Epics, Stories, Bugs, Tasks).
✔ **Customize workflows** to match your development process.
✔ **Assign permissions and roles** appropriately.
✔ **Integrate with developer tools** for seamless collaboration.

With your project set up, the next step is **managing user roles and permissions**, which we'll cover in the next chapter.

User Roles and Permissions for Developer Teams

A well-structured **role and permission system** in Jira is essential for **efficient collaboration, security, and workflow control** within development teams. Without proper permission management, issues can arise, such as unauthorized changes to workflows, confusion over task ownership, and security vulnerabilities.

In this chapter, you will learn:

- **The key Jira roles and their responsibilities**
- **How to configure permissions for development teams**
- **Best practices for setting up permission schemes**
- **How to troubleshoot and manage access control**

By the end of this chapter, you'll have a clear understanding of how to structure roles and permissions in Jira to streamline your development process.

Understanding Jira Roles

Jira uses a **role-based access control (RBAC)** system, where different users are assigned specific roles within a project.

Default Jira Roles

Role	Primary Responsibilities
Administrator	Manages Jira configuration, workflows, and global settings.
Project Lead	Oversees the project, assigns tasks, and manages backlog priorities.
Developer	Works on issues, updates task statuses, and logs work.
QA Tester	Tests resolved issues, reopens defects, and verifies fixes.
Scrum Master	Facilitates sprint planning, ensures agile best practices are followed.
Viewer/Stakeholder	Can view issues but cannot make changes or updates.

Best Practice: Assign roles based on **workflow needs** rather than individual users to ensure consistency in team operations.

Configuring Permissions in Jira

Jira permissions are **configured at the project level** through **Permission Schemes**. Instead of assigning permissions to individual users, Jira allows you to assign them to **roles or groups**, making it easier to manage large teams.

Key Jira Permissions for Development Teams

Jira has over **50 different permissions**, categorized into different types. Below are the most important ones for a development team:

Permission Type	Relevant Permissions	Recommended Role
Project Permissions	Browse Projects, Manage Sprints	Developers, Project Leads
Issue Permissions	Create, Edit, Assign, and Move Issues	Developers, QA, Project Leads
Workflow Permissions	Transition Issues, Reopen Issues	Developers, QA
Comment Permissions	Add, Edit, and Delete Comments	Developers, QA, Stakeholders (View Only)
Attachment Permissions	Add, Edit, and Delete Attachments	Developers, QA
Board Permissions	Manage Board, Configure Filters	Scrum Master, Project Lead

Tip: Use **Jira Groups (e.g., `dev-team`, `qa-team`)** to manage permissions instead of assigning them individually.

Setting Up a Permission Scheme

1. Creating a Custom Permission Scheme

Instead of manually assigning permissions for each project, create a **Permission Scheme** that can be reused across multiple projects.

Steps to Create a Permission Scheme:

1. **Go to Jira Administration → Issues → Permission Schemes**
2. Click **"Create Permission Scheme"**
3. Name your scheme (e.g., **"Software Development Permissions"**)
4. Assign permissions to **roles/groups**
5. Click **Save**

Best Practice: Apply a **single permission scheme** across multiple projects for consistency.

---

2. Assigning Roles to Users

Once the permission scheme is set, assign users to **appropriate roles** in each project.

Steps to Assign a Role to a User:

1. **Go to Jira Project Settings → People**
2. Click **"Add People"**
3. Select a **user or group**
4. Choose a **role** (e.g., Developer, QA, Project Lead)
5. Click **Save**

Best Practice: Assign **groups** instead of individual users to make role management scalable.

Managing User Access Levels

Jira supports multiple access levels to prevent unauthorized changes.

1. Open vs. Restricted Projects

Access Type	Who Can Access?	Best For
Open	Anyone can view and edit issues	Small, non-sensitive projects
Limited	Only selected users can make changes	Development teams with controlled workflows
Private	Only invited users can access the project	High-security or confidential projects

Best Practice: Use **Limited Access** for development teams to prevent unauthorized modifications.

---

2. Restricting Issue Editing

To prevent unwanted changes to issues, set **workflow-based permissions** so only specific roles can edit issues in certain statuses.

Issue Status	Who Can Edit?
Backlog	Project Leads, Developers
In Progress	Developers
Code Review	Developers, Reviewers
QA Testing	QA Testers
Done	Only Admins or Leads

Steps to Restrict Issue Editing:

1. **Go to Jira Administration → Permission Schemes**
2. Select **"Edit Issues" permission**
3. Assign it only to **specific roles (e.g., Developers, Leads)**
4. Click **Save**

Tip: Locking editing for completed issues prevents accidental modifications.

Troubleshooting Common Permission Issues

1. Users Can't See a Project

Possible Cause: They don't have the **Browse Projects** permission.
Solution: Go to **Project Settings → Permissions**, and grant them access.

2. Users Can't Transition Issues

Possible Cause: They don't have the **Transition Issues** permission in the workflow.
Solution: Update **Workflow Permissions** to allow transitions.

3. Team Members Can't Comment on Issues

Possible Cause: Comment permissions are restricted to Admins only.
Solution: Grant **Comment Issue** permission to Developers, QA, and Leads.

4. Developers Can't Move Issues Between Columns in a Kanban Board

Possible Cause: Board settings restrict issue transitions.
Solution: Modify **Board Settings → Column Constraints** to allow movement.

Best Practice: Use **Jira Permission Helper** (Admin → Permission Helper) to debug permission issues quickly.

Best Practices for Managing Roles and Permissions

■ **Use Groups, Not Individual Users** – Assign roles to groups (dev-team, qa-team) instead of individuals for easier management.
■ **Follow Least Privilege Principle** – Grant only the permissions needed for a role.
■ **Limit Issue Editing in Final Stages** – Prevent modifications after tasks are marked as "Done."
■ **Automate Role Assignments** – Use **Jira Automation** to assign roles based on issue type or status.
■ **Audit Permissions Regularly** – Review permission settings periodically to avoid security risks.

Conclusion

Proper **user roles and permissions** management is critical for efficient workflows in Jira. By:

✔ **Defining roles clearly** (Admin, Developer, QA, Scrum Master)
✔ **Using permission schemes** to standardize access
✔ **Assigning permissions based on workflows**
✔ **Troubleshooting common access issues**

…your team can ensure smooth, secure, and efficient collaboration in Jira.

In the next chapter, we'll explore **integrating Jira with development tools** (IDEs, CLI, version control) to further streamline your workflow.

Integrating Jira with Developer Tools (IDEs, CLI)

For development teams, Jira is more than just a task management tool—it's a central hub that connects coding, issue tracking, and deployment processes. To minimize context switching and maximize productivity, developers should integrate Jira with their **Integrated Development Environments (IDEs)** and **Command-Line Interface (CLI) tools**.

This chapter will cover:

- **How to integrate Jira with popular IDEs** (IntelliJ IDEA, VS Code, Eclipse)
- **Using the Jira Command-Line Interface (CLI) for efficiency**
- **Best practices for linking Jira issues to version control and CI/CD pipelines**

By the end of this chapter, you'll be able to manage Jira issues **without leaving your development environment**, reducing friction in your workflow.

Integrating Jira with IDEs

Most modern IDEs offer built-in **Jira integrations** or plugins that allow developers to:

- View assigned issues within the IDE
- Transition issues (move from "To Do" to "In Progress," etc.)
- Create new issues directly from the IDE
- Link commits and pull requests to Jira tickets

1. Integrating Jira with IntelliJ IDEA

JetBrains IDEs, including **IntelliJ IDEA, PyCharm, WebStorm, and Rider**, offer **Jira integration via the built-in Task Management feature**.

Steps to Set Up Jira in IntelliJ IDEA

1. Open **IntelliJ IDEA** and go to **File → Settings → Tools → Tasks & Contexts**.
2. Click **Add** and select **Jira** as the issue tracker.
3. Enter the **Jira URL** (e.g., `https://yourcompany.atlassian.net`).
4. Authenticate using **OAuth, username/password, or API token**.
5. Select your Jira project and click **Test Connection**.
6. Click **OK** to save the integration.

How to Use Jira in IntelliJ IDEA

- **View Assigned Issues** – Go to **View → Tool Windows → Tasks**, then refresh.
- **Work on an Issue** – Select a Jira issue and click **"Start Work"** to create a local branch automatically.
- **Transition Issues** – Right-click an issue and move it from "To Do" to "In Progress" within the IDE.
- **Create a New Jira Issue** – Click **"New Task"**, fill in the details, and create a ticket directly from IntelliJ.

Best Practice: Enable **auto-branching** so that each Jira issue gets a corresponding Git branch (`feature/JIRA-123`).

---

2. Integrating Jira with VS Code

Microsoft's **VS Code** supports Jira integration through extensions such as:

- **Jira and Bitbucket (Atlassian Labs)**
- **Jira Plugin for VS Code**

Steps to Integrate Jira in VS Code

1. Open **VS Code** and go to the **Extensions Marketplace**.
2. Search for **"Jira"** and install the **Jira and Bitbucket (Atlassian Labs)** extension.
3. Go to **Settings → Extensions → Jira** and enter your **Jira instance URL**.
4. Authenticate using **OAuth or API Token**.
5. Reload VS Code to activate the integration.

How to Use Jira in VS Code

- Use the **Jira panel** to view assigned issues.
- Click an issue to open its details and start working on it.
- Use **slash commands (`/jira create`, `/jira transition`)** to manage issues from the command palette.
- Auto-create **Git branches** based on Jira issue names.

Best Practice: Use **VS Code's built-in Git integration** to **link commits to Jira issues** (`JIRA-123 Fix bug` in commit messages).

---

3. Integrating Jira with Eclipse

For developers using **Eclipse**, Jira integration is available via the **Atlassian Connector for Eclipse**.

Steps to Set Up Jira in Eclipse

1. Open **Eclipse** and go to **Help → Eclipse Marketplace**.
2. Search for **"Atlassian Connector for Eclipse"** and install it.
3. Restart Eclipse and go to **Preferences → Task Repositories**.
4. Click **Add Repository** and select **Jira**.
5. Enter your Jira **server URL, username, and password/API token**.
6. Click **Test Connection** and finish the setup.

How to Use Jira in Eclipse

- **Access Jira Issues** – View your assigned tickets from **Task List View**.
- **Work on an Issue** – Select a task and start tracking time within Eclipse.
- **Transition Issues** – Move tickets through Jira workflows directly from the IDE.

Best Practice: If your team uses Bitbucket, enable **Bitbucket integration** for smoother code collaboration.

Using Jira from the Command Line (Jira CLI)

For developers who prefer working in the terminal, the **Jira Command-Line Interface (Jira CLI)** offers a powerful way to interact with Jira without opening the web UI.

1. Installing Jira CLI

To install Jira CLI, use the following command (depending on your OS):

- **Mac/Linux**:

```
brew install jira-cli
```

- **Windows:**
  Download and install from [Jira CLI GitHub Releases] (https://github.com/go-jira/jira/releases).

2. Configuring Jira CLI

After installation, configure Jira CLI by running:

```
jira login
```

Enter your **Jira URL, username, and API token** when prompted.

3. Common Jira CLI Commands

Command	Action
`jira list`	Show all assigned issues
`jira view JIRA-123`	View issue details
`jira transition JIRA-123 "In Progress"`	Move issue to "In Progress"
`jira create -t "Bug" -p DEV -m "Fix login issue"`	Create a new bug
`jira comment JIRA-123 -m "Fixed in latest commit"`	Add a comment to an issue

Best Practice: Alias common Jira commands in your shell (`.bashrc` or `.zshrc`) for quicker access.

Linking Jira to Version Control (GitHub, GitLab, Bitbucket)

To **track development progress**, link Jira issues to Git repositories.

1. Connecting Jira to GitHub/GitLab/Bitbucket

1. **Go to Jira → Project Settings → Development Tools**
2. Select **GitHub, GitLab, or Bitbucket**.
3. Authenticate using **OAuth** or **Personal Access Token**.
4. Enable **auto-linking** of Jira issues to commits and branches.

2. Best Practices for Commit Messages

Use Jira issue keys in commit messages to **automatically link** commits to Jira:

■ **Correct format:**

```
git commit -m "JIRA-123: Fixed authentication bug"
```

■ **Branch Naming:**

```
git checkout -b feature/JIRA-456-user-auth
```

Tip: Set up Jira Automation to **transition issues when pull requests are merged**.

Conclusion

Integrating Jira with **IDEs, CLI tools, and Git repositories** improves developer efficiency by reducing context switching and automating task management.

✔ **Use Jira plugins in IDEs** (IntelliJ, VS Code, Eclipse) for direct access to issues.
✔ **Leverage Jira CLI** for fast terminal-based issue tracking.
✔ **Connect Jira with GitHub, GitLab, or Bitbucket** to link commits, branches, and pull requests.
✔ **Automate transitions** so Jira issues update automatically when code is merged.

In the next chapter, we'll explore **customizing Jira issue types for software projects** to enhance tracking and reporting.

Part 3:
Configuring Jira for Efficiency

Customizing Issue Types for Software Projects

Jira's issue types are the foundation of effective project management in software development. By **customizing issue types**, teams can align Jira with their unique development processes, improving issue tracking, sprint planning, and backlog management.

In this chapter, we'll cover:

- **Default Jira issue types** and their use cases
- **Creating custom issue types** for development workflows
- **Best practices for structuring issue types**
- **Using issue type schemes for different teams**

By the end of this chapter, you'll have a Jira setup tailored to your software projects, allowing for clearer task differentiation and better reporting.

Understanding Default Jira Issue Types

Jira provides several **built-in issue types** for software development teams. These issue types are used to categorize work, making it easier to track progress and prioritize tasks.

Issue Type	Purpose	Typical Use Case
Epic	High-level feature or initiative	"User Authentication System"
Story	A user-focused requirement or feature request	"User should be able to reset password"
Task	General work item that needs completion	"Set up database schema"
Bug	A software defect that needs fixing	"Login page throws 500 error"
Sub-task	A smaller unit of work within a parent issue	"Write unit tests for login module"

These default issue types work well for most teams, but many development projects require additional categories for specialized tracking.

Creating Custom Issue Types

Custom issue types allow teams to define **unique categories** that reflect their workflow. Some common custom issue types include:

Custom Issue Type	Purpose	When to Use
Tech Debt	Tracks refactoring, optimizations, or cleanup work	"Refactor API error handling"
Spike	Research tasks that need investigation	"Evaluate database options for scalability"
Code Review	A ticket for tracking peer code reviews	"Review pull request #123"
Support Request	Internal support tickets within the team	"Set up access to staging environment"
Security Vulnerability	Identifies security risks that need fixing	"Fix SQL injection vulnerability"

Steps to Create a Custom Issue Type

1. **Go to Jira Administration → Issues → Issue Types**
2. Click **"Add Issue Type"**
3. Enter:
   - **Name** (e.g., "Tech Debt")
   - **Description** (e.g., "Refactoring tasks and optimizations")
   - **Type**: Choose between **Standard Issue** or **Sub-task**
4. Click **Save**

Now, your new issue type can be added to projects and workflows.

Assigning Issue Types to Projects

Once you've created custom issue types, they need to be assigned to **issue type schemes** so they are available in relevant projects.

What Is an Issue Type Scheme?

An **issue type scheme** determines which issue types are available in a given project.

For example, a **Backend Development Project** might have:
- Bugs
- Stories
- Tasks
- Tech Debt

While a **QA Testing Project** might include:
- Bugs
- Test Cases
- Exploratory Testing

Best Practice: Assign different issue type schemes to backend, frontend, and QA teams to keep Jira organized.

Steps to Assign an Issue Type Scheme

1. **Go to Jira Administration → Issues → Issue Type Schemes**
2. Click **"Create Issue Type Scheme"**
3. Add the relevant issue types to the scheme
4. Assign the scheme to one or more projects

Best Practices for Structuring Issue Types

1. Keep It Simple

Avoid adding too many issue types—**3 to 7 issue types per project** is ideal.

■ **Good Example:**

- Epic
- Story
- Bug
- Task
- Sub-task

✗ **Bad Example:**

- Epic
- Feature
- Story
- Enhancement
- Defect
- Hotfix
- Tech Debt
- Code Review
- Maintenance

2. Use Issue Hierarchies for Better Tracking

Jira's issue hierarchy helps break down work into **manageable levels**:

Epic → Story/Task → Sub-task

- **Epics** track major features or initiatives.
- **Stories and tasks** break down epics into smaller, actionable units.
- **Sub-tasks** divide tasks into specific steps.

Tip: Use **Jira Advanced Roadmaps** to visualize dependencies between issue types.

3. Automate Issue Type Assignments

To streamline issue management, use **Jira Automation** to **assign issue types dynamically**:

■ Automatically classify bugs
■ Convert "urgent" issues into **Hotfixes**
■ Create **Code Review** tasks when a pull request is submitted

Example Automation Rule:

- **Trigger:** A new issue is created
- **Condition:** If issue contains "research" in the summary
- **Action:** Change issue type to **Spike**

Using Custom Fields to Enhance Issue Types

In addition to creating **custom issue types**, adding **custom fields** improves issue tracking.

Common Custom Fields for Development Teams

Field Name	Field Type	Use Case
Code Review Status	Dropdown (Pending, Approved, Rejected)	Tracks code review progress
Tech Debt Level	Dropdown (Low, Medium, High)	Prioritizes refactoring tasks
Environment	Dropdown (Development, Staging, Production)	Identifies where a bug occurred
Root Cause	Text field	Stores debugging insights

Steps to Add a Custom Field

1. **Go to Jira Administration → Issues → Custom Fields**
2. Click **"Create Custom Field"**
3. Choose a **field type** (Dropdown, Text, Checkbox, etc.)
4. Name the field (e.g., "Tech Debt Level")
5. Assign it to **relevant issue types** (e.g., Tech Debt, Bug)

Now, every time an issue is created, these custom fields will be available.

Reporting and Analytics for Custom Issue Types

Jira's reporting features can be customized based on issue types to provide **valuable insights**.

1. Custom Dashboards

■ **Tech Debt Overview:** Show the number of **open vs. resolved tech debt issues**
■ **Bug Trend Analysis:** Track the frequency of new bugs over time
■ **Code Review Metrics:** Measure how many reviews are pending

2. JQL Queries for Custom Issue Types

Jira Query Language (JQL) allows teams to filter issues by custom issue types:

- **Find all open Tech Debt issues:**

```
project = DEV AND issuetype = "Tech Debt" AND status != Done
```

- **List all unresolved security vulnerabilities:**

```
project = SECURITY AND issuetype = "Security Vulnerability" AND
resolution = Unresolved
```

- **Track spikes completed in the last 30 days**:

```
issuetype = Spike AND status = Done AND updated >= -30d
```

Best Practice: Save JQL filters as **custom Jira dashboards** for quick access.

Conclusion

Customizing **Jira issue types** is essential for **optimizing software development workflows**.

✔ Use **custom issue types** (Tech Debt, Spike, Code Review) for better organization.
✔ Assign issue types **strategically** to different teams (Frontend, Backend, QA).
✔ Automate issue classification with **Jira Automation**.
✔ Add **custom fields** to improve tracking (e.g., Review Status, Root Cause).
✔ Leverage **JQL filters and dashboards** for better reporting.

With the right issue type setup, Jira becomes a **powerful tool for development teams**, enabling clearer tracking, improved productivity, and streamlined project management.

Designing Agile-Friendly Workflows

Agile software development thrives on flexibility, iteration, and continuous improvement. To fully leverage Jira in an Agile environment, teams need well-designed **workflows** that align with their development practices.

A well-structured **Jira workflow** ensures that:

- Tasks move smoothly from **backlog to completion**
- Developers, testers, and product managers **collaborate seamlessly**
- Teams **track progress efficiently** without bottlenecks

In this chapter, we'll cover:

- **Understanding Agile workflows (Scrum vs. Kanban)**
- **Creating and customizing workflows in Jira**
- **Best practices for Agile development teams**
- **Automating workflow transitions** for efficiency

By the end of this chapter, you'll be able to create **custom workflows in Jira** that streamline software development and improve team efficiency.

Understanding Agile Workflows

1. Scrum vs. Kanban: Choosing the Right Workflow

Agile teams typically use **Scrum or Kanban** (or a hybrid of both) to manage their development workflow. Jira supports both methodologies through **configurable workflows**.

Scrum Workflow (Sprint-Based)

- Work is planned in **sprints** (1-4 weeks)
- Tasks move through predefined statuses within the sprint
- Teams review progress in **standups and sprint retrospectives**

Example Scrum Workflow

Backlog → Selected for Development → In Progress → Code Review → QA Testing → Done

■ **Best for:** Feature development, structured teams, time-boxed iterations

---

Kanban Workflow (Continuous Flow)

- Tasks move through **work-in-progress (WIP) limits**
- There are **no fixed sprints**—work is continuously deployed
- Helps visualize bottlenecks using a **Kanban board**

Example Kanban Workflow

Backlog → In Progress → Code Review → Ready for Release → Done

■ **Best for:** DevOps teams, bug tracking, continuous delivery

Hybrid Approach: Many teams combine Scrum and Kanban (**Scrumban**)—using sprints while maintaining a **continuous backlog**.

Creating a Custom Jira Workflow

1. Understanding Jira Workflow Components

A Jira workflow consists of:

Component	Purpose	Example
Statuses	Represents where a task is in the workflow	"To Do," "In Progress," "Done"
Transitions	Defines how an issue moves between statuses	"Move to Code Review"
Conditions	Restricts who can perform certain transitions	"Only Developers can move to 'Done'"
Validators	Ensures certain conditions are met before transitioning	"Code must be reviewed before moving to QA"
Post Functions	Automates actions when an issue moves to a new status	"Assign issue to QA automatically"

2. Steps to Create a Custom Workflow in Jira

Step 1: Navigate to Jira Workflows

- Go to **Jira Administration → Issues → Workflows**
- Click **Create New Workflow**

Step 2: Define Workflow Statuses

- Add statuses based on your Agile process (**To Do, In Progress, Code Review, QA Testing, Done**)
- Use **color coding** to differentiate stages visually

Step 3: Add Transitions Between Statuses

- Connect statuses using **arrows**
- Ensure logical flow:

  Backlog → In Progress → Code Review → QA Testing → Done

Step 4: Apply Conditions and Validators

- Example: **Only QA can move issues from "Testing" to "Done"**
- Add a validator to ensure **"Code Review" is completed before testing**

Step 5: Save and Activate the Workflow

- Assign the workflow to your **Software Development project**
- Test transitions to ensure the flow works smoothly

Best Practices for Agile Workflows in Jira

1. Keep Workflows Simple and Focused

◼ Use **3-7 statuses** to avoid complexity
◼ Ensure **logical transitions** (e.g., Code Review → QA, not directly to Done)
◼ Don't overload workflows with unnecessary custom rules

2. Automate Workflow Transitions

Jira Automation can **reduce manual updates** and enforce Agile best practices.

◼ **Automatically move issues when a branch is created**

Example Rule:

- **Trigger:** A new Git branch is created with a Jira issue key
- **Action:** Move the issue to **"In Progress"**

◼ **Move issues to "Done" when pull requests are merged**

Example Rule:

- **Trigger:** A pull request is merged in GitHub
- **Action:** Move Jira issue from "Code Review" → "Done"

◼ **Send Slack notifications when tasks move to "Blocked"**

Example Rule:

- **Trigger:** Issue status changes to **"Blocked"**
- **Action:** Send an alert to the **#dev-team** Slack channel

Tip: Use **Jira's If-This-Then-That (IFTTT) rules** to streamline transitions.

3. Enforce WIP Limits for Kanban

Work-In-Progress (WIP) limits prevent teams from **overloading their backlog**.

◼ Set a **maximum of 3 issues per developer** in "In Progress"
◼ Limit "Code Review" to **5 issues at a time** to prevent bottlenecks

How to Set WIP Limits in Jira

1. **Go to Board Settings → Columns**
2. Enable **Work In Progress (WIP) Limits**
3. Set max limits for each column (e.g., **3 issues per dev**)

4. Use Swimlanes for Prioritization

Swimlanes help **categorize tasks visually**.

Example Swimlanes

- **High Priority Bugs** → Urgent defects
- **Feature Development** → Planned stories
- **Tech Debt** → Refactoring work

Best Practice: Use **JQL Queries** to define swimlane filters dynamically.

Example Jira Workflow Configurations

1. Basic Scrum Workflow

Statuses:
■ Backlog → Selected for Development → In Progress → Code Review → QA Testing → Done

■ **Transitions:**

- Developers **move issues from "Backlog" to "In Progress"**
- Pull requests **automatically trigger "Code Review"**
- QA testers **move issues from "QA Testing" to "Done"**

---

2. Advanced Kanban Workflow

Statuses:
■ Backlog → In Progress → Code Review → Ready for Release → Done

■ **Automation Rules:**

- Auto-assign issues in **"Ready for Release"** to the deployment team
- Limit **"Code Review" column to max 5 issues**
- Notify the team when an issue gets stuck in "Blocked"

Conclusion

Designing an **Agile-friendly workflow** in Jira helps software teams:

✔ Reduce **manual work** with **automated transitions**
✔ Improve **team efficiency** by limiting WIP and enforcing review processes
✔ Streamline **collaboration** by ensuring proper role-based transitions

By customizing your Jira workflow, you **eliminate friction**, improve **sprint velocity**, and enable a **more efficient development process**.

Setting Up Sprints and Epics in Jira

Sprints and epics are **fundamental to Agile development**. Properly structuring them in Jira allows teams to manage large-scale projects efficiently, break down work into manageable units, and track progress effectively.

In this chapter, you'll learn:

- **The difference between epics, stories, and tasks**
- **How to set up sprints and manage backlog items**
- **Best practices for sprint planning in Jira**
- **How to track sprint progress and retrospectives**

By the end of this chapter, your team will be able to use **Jira sprints and epics** to improve development velocity and ensure smooth delivery cycles.

Understanding Epics, Stories, and Sprints

1. What Are Epics in Jira?

Epics represent **large features or projects** that require multiple sprints to complete. They help teams **group related stories and tasks** under a single umbrella.

Epic	Definition	Example
Large Feature	A big development effort that spans multiple sprints	"User Authentication System"
Initiative	A high-level goal that includes several related epics	"Redesign entire frontend UI"

Tip: Epics should be broken down into **smaller, actionable user stories** to be completed within a sprint.

2. What Are Stories and Tasks?

Issue Type	Purpose	Example
Story	A user requirement or feature request	"Users should be able to reset passwords"
Task	A technical implementation required to complete a story	"Implement API endpoint for password reset"
Sub-task	A smaller piece of a task	"Write unit tests for API"

Best Practice: Use **stories for user-focused work** and **tasks for development work** that doesn't directly impact the user.

3. What Are Sprints in Jira?

A **sprint** is a time-boxed iteration (1-4 weeks) where teams complete planned stories and tasks.

Sprint Term	Definition
Sprint Planning	A meeting where the team selects work for the sprint
Sprint Goal	A clear objective that defines the sprint's success
Sprint Backlog	A prioritized list of stories/tasks for the sprint
Sprint Retrospective	A meeting to review what went well and what needs improvement

Tip: Sprints should be **consistent in length** (e.g., 2 weeks) for predictable delivery cycles.

Setting Up Epics in Jira

1. Creating an Epic in Jira

Steps to Create an Epic:

1. **Go to the Backlog** in your Jira project
2. Click **Create Issue → Select "Epic" as the Issue Type**
3. Enter a **Title** (e.g., "User Authentication System")
4. Add a **Description** (e.g., "Implement login, registration, and password reset features")
5. Click **Create**

Adding Stories to an Epic

1. Open the **Backlog**
2. Drag and drop existing stories into the epic
3. Or create a new story and **select an Epic Link**

Best Practice: Keep **epics limited to a few sprints**—if an epic grows too large, break it into multiple smaller epics.

Setting Up Sprints in Jira

1. Creating a Sprint

1. **Go to the Backlog View**
2. Click **"Create Sprint"**
3. Name your sprint (e.g., **Sprint 5: Login Feature**)
4. Drag and drop issues from the backlog into the sprint
5. Click **"Start Sprint"**

Sprint Best Practices

■ **Sprint length should be consistent** (1-4 weeks)
■ **Include only as much work as the team can handle**
■ **Define a clear sprint goal**
■ **Use story points or estimates to gauge workload**

Managing Sprint Backlogs

A **well-maintained backlog** ensures that teams work on the most critical tasks first.

1. Prioritizing the Sprint Backlog

Priority Level	Type of Work	Example
High	Critical features, bug fixes	"Fix payment gateway failure"
Medium	Important but non-blocking tasks	"Optimize database queries"
Low	Minor improvements	"Update error messages for clarity"

■ **Use Jira's drag-and-drop feature** to order backlog items based on priority.
■ **Add labels like** `urgent` **or** `blocker` to highlight high-priority work.

2. Using Story Points for Estimation

- Assign **story points** to each issue based on **complexity** (not hours).
- Use **Fibonacci sequence (1, 2, 3, 5, 8, 13)** for estimates.
- Example:
  - **1-3 points:** Small bug fixes
  - **5-8 points:** Medium-sized feature
  - **13+ points:** Large feature requiring multiple developers

Tip: If an issue is **13+ points**, break it into smaller stories.

Tracking Sprint Progress

1. Using Jira's Active Sprint Board

- **To Do → In Progress → Code Review → QA → Done**
- Drag issues across columns to reflect progress
- Monitor WIP (Work In Progress) limits to **avoid bottlenecks**

2. Sprint Reports and Metrics

Report	Purpose
Burndown Chart	Shows remaining work in the sprint
Velocity Chart	Measures how much work is completed per sprint
Sprint Report	Provides a summary of completed vs. incomplete tasks

■ Use **burndown charts** to track sprint progress.
■ Analyze **velocity trends** to improve sprint planning.

Sprint Reviews and Retrospectives

1. Sprint Review (Demo Day)

- Showcase completed work to stakeholders
- Ensure features meet **Acceptance Criteria**

2. Sprint Retrospective

What went well?
What could be improved?
What will we change in the next sprint?

▪ Keep retrospectives **short (30-60 min)**
▪ Use Jira's **Retrospective Report** to track past feedback

Common Pitfalls and How to Avoid Them

Issue	Solution
Overloaded Sprint	Use **story points** to ensure realistic workloads
No Clear Sprint Goal	Define sprint objectives before starting
Scope Creep	Lock sprint backlog after sprint starts
Issues Not Moving	Set WIP limits and automate workflow transitions

Conclusion

Setting up **sprints and epics** properly in Jira enables Agile teams to:

✔ Plan **manageable iterations**
✔ Prioritize **critical features first**
✔ Track **progress with velocity and burndown reports**
✔ Improve efficiency through **retrospectives**

By following these best practices, your team will **increase productivity and deliver software faster**.

Configuring Boards (Scrum, Kanban) for Your Team

Jira's boards are essential for **visualizing work, tracking progress, and managing Agile workflows** efficiently. Whether your team follows **Scrum or Kanban**, configuring boards properly ensures that development stays organized and productive.

In this chapter, you'll learn:

- **The difference between Scrum and Kanban boards**
- **How to create and configure a Jira board**
- **Best practices for board customization**
- **Using Jira boards for sprint planning and backlog management**
- **Optimizing boards with filters, columns, and automation**

By the end of this chapter, you'll have a fully functional **Scrum or Kanban board** tailored to your team's workflow.

Understanding Scrum and Kanban Boards

1. Scrum Boards (Sprint-Based Workflow)

A **Scrum board** is used by teams that work in **sprints (1-4 weeks)** and need to track work from backlog to completion.

■ **Best for:**

- Teams that plan work in iterations (sprints)
- Development teams with structured planning
- Feature development and new product releases

■ **Scrum Board Features:**

- Sprint backlog with prioritized issues
- Drag-and-drop workflow for tracking work
- Sprint reports (burndown, velocity, completed vs. incomplete work)

Example Scrum Workflow:
Backlog → Selected for Sprint → In Progress → Code Review → QA Testing → Done

---

2. Kanban Boards (Continuous Workflow)

A **Kanban board** is used for **continuous delivery and real-time tracking**, without fixed sprints.

■ **Best for:**

- DevOps and support teams
- Bug tracking and maintenance work
- Teams that don't follow sprint planning

■ **Kanban Board Features:**

- Work-in-progress (WIP) limits to prevent overloading
- Continuous workflow without sprint constraints
- Cycle time tracking for issue resolution

Example Kanban Workflow:
Backlog → In Progress → Code Review → Ready for Release → Done

Choosing Between Scrum and Kanban:

- Use **Scrum** if your team works in sprints with structured planning.
- Use **Kanban** if your team focuses on continuous flow and minimizing lead time.

Creating a Jira Board

1. Steps to Create a Scrum Board

1. **Go to Jira → Click "Boards" → Create Board**
2. Select **Scrum Board**
3. Choose to create a board **from an existing project** or **from scratch**
4. Name your board (e.g., **"Frontend Team Scrum"**)
5. Assign it to your team's Jira project

2. Steps to Create a Kanban Board

1. **Go to Jira → Click "Boards" → Create Board**
2. Select **Kanban Board**
3. Choose to create a board **from an existing project** or **from scratch**
4. Name your board (e.g., **"DevOps Kanban"**)
5. Assign it to your team's Jira project

Best Practice: Use different boards for **Frontend, Backend, and QA teams** to prevent clutter in a single board.

Customizing Your Jira Board

1. Configuring Board Columns

Jira boards display **work items in columns** representing different workflow stages.

■ **Scrum Board Columns Example:**

Column Name	Description
Backlog	Unprioritized tasks for future sprints
To Do	Sprint backlog (tasks planned for the current sprint)
In Progress	Active development work

Code Review	Peer reviews before merging changes
QA Testing	Tasks being tested before release
Done	Completed work ready for release

■ **Kanban Board Columns Example:**

Column Name	Description
Backlog	Unprioritized tasks
In Progress	Active development work
Blocked	Tasks waiting on external dependencies
Ready for Release	Work completed but not deployed
Done	Released and fully implemented work

Tip: Use **WIP (Work In Progress) Limits** to **prevent bottlenecks**—for example, limit "Code Review" to a **maximum of 5 issues** at a time.

---

2. Using Quick Filters for Better Navigation

Quick filters allow teams to **customize board views** for better focus.

Filter Name	JQL Query	Purpose
My Tasks	`assignee = currentUser()`	Shows only tasks assigned to the logged-in user
High Priority	`priority = High`	Highlights urgent tasks
Bugs Only	`issuetype = Bug`	Filters out non-bug issues
Ready for Testing	`status = "Code Review"`	Displays tasks awaiting QA testing

How to Set Up Quick Filters in Jira

1. **Go to Board Settings → Quick Filters**
2. Click **"Add Filter"**
3. Enter a **name and JQL query**
4. Click **Save**

Best Practice: Encourage teams to use **Quick Filters** for faster navigation and prioritization.

Managing Workflows on Jira Boards

1. Automating Workflow Transitions

To reduce **manual updates**, use Jira Automation to **automate issue transitions**:

■ **Auto-move issues to "In Progress" when a branch is created**

Example Rule:

- **Trigger:** A new Git branch is created with a Jira issue key
- **Action:** Move the issue to **"In Progress"**

■ **Move issues to "Done" when pull requests are merged**

Example Rule:

- **Trigger:** A pull request is merged in GitHub
- **Action:** Move Jira issue from "Code Review" → "Done"

■ **Send Slack notifications when tasks move to "Blocked"**

Example Rule:

- **Trigger:** Issue status changes to **"Blocked"**
- **Action:** Send an alert to the **#dev-team** Slack channel

---

Sprint Planning and Tracking

For Scrum teams, the board helps with **sprint planning** and tracking sprint progress.

1. Planning a Sprint in Jira

1. Open **Scrum Board** → **Backlog View**
2. Select high-priority stories and tasks
3. Move them to **Sprint Backlog**
4. Define a **Sprint Goal**
5. Click **"Start Sprint"**

2. Tracking Sprint Progress

- Use **Burndown Charts** to track remaining work
- Monitor **Velocity Reports** to predict team performance
- Ensure **unfinished work is moved to the next sprint**

Best Practices for Optimizing Jira Boards

✔ **Keep Workflows Simple** – Avoid unnecessary columns and status transitions
✔ **Use WIP Limits** – Prevent overloading developers with too many active tasks
✔ **Set Clear Sprint Goals** – Ensure each sprint has a well-defined objective
✔ **Use Labels and Components** – Categorize work for better filtering
✔ **Regularly Archive Done Issues** – Keep boards clean and fast

---

Conclusion

Jira boards are **powerful tools** for tracking and managing Agile development workflows. By:

✔ Choosing the right board **(Scrum for sprints, Kanban for continuous work)**
✔ Configuring **columns, quick filters, and automation rules**
✔ Managing **workflows efficiently** and reducing manual updates
✔ Tracking **sprint progress through reports and burndown charts**

…your team will have **a clear, efficient system for managing work in Jira**.

Automating Repetitive Tasks with Jira Automation

Manual task updates in Jira can slow down development teams and introduce inefficiencies. **Jira Automation** helps streamline workflows by **eliminating repetitive tasks**, reducing administrative overhead, and improving consistency in issue tracking.

With Jira Automation, you can:

- **Auto-assign issues** based on conditions
- **Move issues between statuses** automatically
- **Trigger notifications** for key events
- **Integrate Jira with CI/CD pipelines and development tools**

In this chapter, you'll learn:

- **How Jira Automation works**
- **Creating automation rules for common developer tasks**
- **Using smart values for dynamic issue updates**
- **Best practices for optimizing Jira Automation**

By the end of this chapter, you'll be able to **automate your Jira workflows**, improving efficiency and reducing manual work.

Understanding Jira Automation

1. What Is Jira Automation?

Jira Automation is a **rule-based system** that allows teams to set up **If-This-Then-That (IFTTT)** workflows, where:

- **Trigger:** An event that starts the rule (e.g., issue created, pull request merged).
- **Condition:** A rule that must be met before the action runs (e.g., issue type = Bug).
- **Action:** What Jira should do (e.g., assign issue, transition status, send notification).

Example: When a **pull request is merged in GitHub**, automatically **move the linked Jira issue to "Done"**.

Creating Your First Automation Rule

1. How to Access Jira Automation

1. **Go to Project Settings → Automation**
2. Click **"Create Rule"**
3. Choose a **Trigger**
4. Add **Conditions (optional)**
5. Define an **Action**
6. Click **Save & Activate**

Common Jira Automation Rules for Developers

1. Automatically Assign Issues to Developers

Use Case: When a new issue is created, auto-assign it based on labels.

Rule Setup:

- **Trigger:** Issue Created
- **Condition:** If label = frontend → Assign to Frontend Dev
- **Action:** Auto-assign issue

JQL Condition Example:

```
labels = "frontend"
```

Alternative: Use **Round Robin Assignment** to distribute issues evenly among developers.

2. Move Issues to "In Progress" When a Branch Is Created

Use Case: When a developer starts working on an issue and creates a Git branch, the issue should move to "In Progress".

Rule Setup:

- **Trigger:** Branch Created (GitHub, GitLab, Bitbucket)
- **Condition:** Issue Status = "To Do"
- **Action:** Move issue to **In Progress**

Tip: Ensure your Jira project is **integrated with your repository** to enable automation.

3. Auto-Close Issues When a Pull Request Is Merged

Use Case: Once a pull request is merged, mark the issue as **"Done"**.

Rule Setup:

- **Trigger:** Pull Request Merged
- **Condition:** Issue Status = "In Code Review"
- **Action:** Move issue to **Done**

JQL for Filtering PR-Linked Issues:

```
development[pullrequests].open > 0
```

Best Practice: Add a **comment in Jira** saying, "This issue was closed because the associated PR was merged."

4. Notify Slack When an Issue Becomes Blocked

Use Case: If a developer moves an issue to "Blocked," send a Slack notification to the team.

Rule Setup:

- **Trigger:** Issue Status Changes to "Blocked"
- **Action:** Send a Slack message to #dev-team

Example Slack Message:

🔔 Issue BLOCKED: {{issue.key}} - {{issue.summary}}.
Please check: {{issue.url}}

Best Practice: Use automation to also **add a "Blocked" label** for better tracking.

---

5. Remind Developers About Stale Issues

■ **Use Case:** If an issue stays in "In Progress" for **more than 5 days**, remind the developer.

Rule Setup:

- **Trigger:** Scheduled (Daily Check)
- **Condition:** Issues in "In Progress" for **>5 days**
- **Action:** Send an email to the assignee

JQL for Finding Stale Issues:

```
status = "In Progress" AND updated < -5d
```

Tip: You can also notify the **Scrum Master** or **Project Lead** about stale issues.

Using Smart Values for Dynamic Updates

Jira provides **Smart Values** that allow automation rules to dynamically pull in **issue details**.

■ **Common Smart Values:**

Smart Value	Usage	Example Output
`{{issue.key}}`	Jira issue key	`JIRA-123`
`{{issue.summary}}`	Issue title	`Fix login bug`
`{{issue.url}}`	Direct link to issue	`https://yourjira.com/JIRA-123`
`{{issue.assignee.displayName}}`	Assignee name	`John Doe`
`{{issue.status.name}}`	Current issue status	`In Progress`

■ **Example: Automatically Add a Comment When a Task Moves to "QA"**

Testing has started on **{{issue.summary}}** ({{{issue.key}}}).
Assigned QA: **{{issue.assignee.displayName}}**.

Best Practices for Jira Automation

1. Keep Rules Simple

■ Avoid **complex nested conditions**—break them into separate rules
■ Start with **basic rules** and add complexity gradually

2. Avoid Too Many Notifications

■ **Limit Slack and Email alerts** to only critical updates
■ Use **JQL to filter unnecessary notifications**

3. Regularly Audit Automation Rules

■ Review **automation logs** for **failed or inefficient rules**
■ **Disable unused rules** to keep automation clean

4. Combine Automation with Webhooks

■ Trigger external actions, like **CI/CD pipelines or deployment scripts**

Conclusion

Jira Automation is a **powerful tool** for streamlining software development workflows by:

✔ **Auto-assigning issues** to the right developers
✔ **Moving tasks automatically** based on repository actions
✔ **Reducing manual updates** for status changes
✔ **Notifying teams instantly** about important issues

By implementing these automation rules, teams can **save time, reduce errors, and improve Jira efficiency**.

Custom Fields and Screens for Tracking Technical Debt

Technical debt accumulates when teams prioritize fast delivery over long-term code maintainability. While some technical debt is inevitable, **tracking and managing it effectively in Jira** ensures that it doesn't become a bottleneck.

Jira's **custom fields and screens** allow teams to:

■ **Categorize technical debt** for better prioritization
■ **Capture metadata like severity, estimated effort, and impact**
■ **Ensure visibility** into technical debt for decision-making

In this chapter, we'll cover:

- **Why tracking technical debt matters**
- **How to create custom fields for technical debt issues**
- **Setting up custom screens for better issue tracking**
- **Best practices for managing technical debt in Jira**

By the end of this chapter, your team will have a structured way to **identify, track, and resolve technical debt** efficiently.

Understanding Technical Debt in Jira

1. What Is Technical Debt?

Technical debt refers to **suboptimal code, architecture, or processes** that require future refactoring. It usually results from:

- **Shortcuts taken to meet deadlines**
- **Lack of documentation or testing**
- **Outdated frameworks and dependencies**

Types of Technical Debt

Type	Description	Example
Code Debt	Poorly structured code that needs refactoring	"Spaghetti code with no modularization"
Design Debt	Architectural decisions that cause inefficiencies	"Monolithic design instead of microservices"
Testing Debt	Lack of unit/integration tests	"No automated test coverage for critical features"
Documentation Debt	Missing or outdated documentation	"No API documentation for external services"
Infrastructure Debt	Outdated tools and dependencies	"Using an unsupported database version"

Best Practice: Use Jira to **classify and track technical debt separately** from feature development.

Creating Custom Fields for Technical Debt

Jira's **custom fields** allow teams to **add specific attributes** to technical debt issues.

1. Common Custom Fields for Technical Debt

Field Name	Field Type	Purpose
Debt Type	Dropdown (Code, Design, Testing, etc.)	Categorizes technical debt
Impact Level	Dropdown (Low, Medium, High, Critical)	Measures severity
Estimated Effort	Numeric (Story Points, Hours)	Helps with prioritization
Root Cause	Text Field	Captures why the debt exists
Refactoring Deadline	Date Field	Sets a deadline for resolution

2. Steps to Create a Custom Field in Jira

1. **Go to Jira Administration → Issues → Custom Fields**
2. Click **"Create Custom Field"**
3. Choose a **field type** (Dropdown, Text, Number, Date)
4. Enter **Field Name** (e.g., "Debt Type")
5. Configure **field options** (e.g., "Code, Design, Testing")
6. Assign the field to **Technical Debt issue types**
7. Click **Save and Apply**

■ **Now, your technical debt issues will have these additional attributes** for better tracking.

Creating a Custom Screen for Technical Debt

A **custom screen** allows teams to **display only relevant fields** for technical debt issues.

1. Steps to Create a Custom Screen

1. **Go to Jira Administration → Issues → Screens**
2. Click **"Create New Screen"**
3. Name it **"Technical Debt Screen"**
4. Add relevant custom fields:
   - ■ Debt Type
   - ■ Impact Level
   - ■ Estimated Effort
   - ■ Root Cause
   - ■ Refactoring Deadline
5. Click **Save and Associate the Screen with an Issue Type**

■ Now, whenever a technical debt issue is created, the custom screen ensures that relevant details are captured.

Managing Technical Debt with Jira Workflows

1. Setting Up a Workflow for Technical Debt

A **custom workflow** for technical debt helps teams manage and prioritize refactoring efforts.

Recommended Workflow:
Identified → Prioritized → In Progress → Code Review → Resolved

■ **Add workflow conditions:**

- Only **Tech Leads** can move issues from **Prioritized** → **In Progress**
- Auto-assign issues to **senior developers** for review
- Notify the **Scrum Master** when an issue stays in **"Identified" for too long**

Best Practice: Use Jira Automation to **auto-tag issues with high impact** for immediate attention.

Tracking and Reporting on Technical Debt

1. Creating a Technical Debt Dashboard

A **custom Jira dashboard** can help teams **monitor technical debt trends**.

Key Dashboard Widgets

■ **Technical Debt Overview** – Show total unresolved debt issues
■ **Debt by Impact Level** – Display a pie chart for Low/Medium/High impact debts
■ **Debt Resolution Trend** – Track how quickly debt is being resolved
■ **Debt Assigned to Teams** – Filter debt by Backend, Frontend, DevOps

2. Using JQL to Filter Technical Debt

Jira Query Language (**JQL**) can be used to **generate reports on technical debt**.

■ **Find all unresolved technical debt issues:**

```
issuetype = "Technical Debt" AND status != Done
```

■ **List all high-impact technical debt items:**

```
issuetype = "Technical Debt" AND Impact Level = High
```

■ **Find technical debt older than 6 months:**

```
issuetype = "Technical Debt" AND created <= -180d
```

■ **Track overdue refactoring tasks:**

```
issuetype = "Technical Debt" AND "Refactoring Deadline" < now()
```

Best Practice: Use these **JQL filters in dashboards** to improve visibility.

Best Practices for Managing Technical Debt in Jira

■ 1. Make Technical Debt Visible

- Create a **dedicated Jira board** for tracking debt
- Use labels like **tech-debt, refactor-needed**

■ 2. Prioritize and Plan for Refactoring

- Use **Impact Level** and **Estimated Effort** fields to prioritize
- Dedicate **10-20% of each sprint** for technical debt resolution

■ 3. Link Technical Debt to Features and Bugs

- Use **issue links** to connect tech debt with related stories
- Add comments explaining **how tech debt affects functionality**

■ 4. Regularly Review and Clean Up Old Debt

- Run JQL reports to **identify outdated or irrelevant debt**
- Close debt that is **no longer relevant due to system updates**

■ 5. Automate Notifications for Unresolved Debt

- Use Jira Automation to **remind the team about overdue tech debt**
- Notify leads when debt is **not updated for more than 30 days**

Conclusion

Using **custom fields and screens**, teams can track **technical debt systematically** in Jira. By:

- ✔ **Creating fields for impact, effort, and root cause**
- ✔ **Setting up custom screens for better visibility**
- ✔ **Building workflows to prioritize and resolve debt**
- ✔ **Using JQL queries and dashboards to monitor trends**

...your team can ensure that **technical debt is managed proactively, not ignored**.

Part 4:
Advanced Workflow Management

Prioritizing Backlogs for Maximum Productivity

A well-managed backlog ensures that development teams work on **the most valuable tasks first** while maintaining a structured workflow. Without proper prioritization, teams risk working on **low-impact features**, accumulating **unresolved bugs**, and slowing down **product delivery**.

In this chapter, you'll learn:

- **The role of a backlog in Agile development**
- **How to prioritize issues using proven techniques**
- **Using Jira backlog features effectively**
- **Best practices for maintaining a healthy backlog**

By the end of this chapter, you'll be able to **optimize your backlog for efficiency, reduce clutter, and improve sprint planning**.

Understanding the Backlog in Jira

1. What Is a Backlog?

The **backlog** is a dynamic list of tasks, user stories, and technical improvements that are waiting to be worked on. It serves as the **single source of truth** for the development team.

■ **Scrum Teams:** The backlog feeds into the **sprint backlog**, which contains tasks planned for a sprint.
■ **Kanban Teams:** The backlog is continuously refined, with the most urgent tasks pulled into **In Progress**.

2. Why Backlog Prioritization Matters

- **Ensures high-impact work is completed first**
- **Prevents backlog bloat and irrelevant tasks**
- **Improves sprint planning and team efficiency**
- **Balances feature development with bug fixes and technical debt**

Backlog Prioritization Techniques

1. MoSCoW Method

The **MoSCoW framework** classifies backlog items into four categories:

Category	Definition	Example

Must Have	Critical features that must be delivered	"User authentication system"
Should Have	Important but not urgent	"Dark mode UI option"
Could Have	Nice-to-have features	"Customizable dashboard themes"
Won't Have	Low-priority or out-of-scope items	"AI-based chatbot for customer support"

■ **How to Use in Jira:**

- Add a **Custom Field** for MoSCoW prioritization.
- Filter backlog issues based on **Must Have** items for sprint planning.

---

2. Value vs. Effort Matrix

Plot backlog items based on **business value vs. implementation effort**:

■ **Quick Wins (High Value, Low Effort):** Prioritize for upcoming sprints.
■ **Strategic Investments (High Value, High Effort):** Plan for future sprints.
■ **Low-Hanging Fruit (Low Value, Low Effort):** Do when time allows.
■ **Avoid (Low Value, High Effort):** Consider removing from backlog.

Using Jira Custom Fields for Value vs. Effort

- Add **two custom fields**: **Business Value (1-5)** and **Effort Estimate (Story Points)**.
- Create Jira filters to identify **Quick Wins**.

Example JQL Query for Quick Wins:

```
"Business Value" >= 4 AND "Effort Estimate" <= 3
```

---

3. Weighted Shortest Job First (WSJF)

WSJF helps prioritize tasks based on the highest return on investment. The formula:

WSJF = (Business Value + Time Criticality + Risk Reduction) / Effort

Steps to Implement in Jira

1. Add custom fields:
   - **Business Value (1-5)**
   - **Time Sensitivity (1-5)**
   - **Risk Reduction (1-5)**
   - **Effort Estimate (Story Points)**
2. Calculate WSJF automatically using Jira Automation.
3. Sort backlog based on **highest WSJF score**.

---

4. Eisenhower Matrix (Urgent vs. Important)

Categorize tasks as:

■ **Do Now (Urgent & Important)** → Move to the next sprint.
■ **Schedule (Not Urgent, Important)** → Plan for future sprints.
■ **Delegate (Urgent, Not Important)** → Assign to appropriate team members.
■ **Eliminate (Not Urgent, Not Important)** → Remove from the backlog.

■ **How to Use in Jira:**

- Label issues as **Urgent, Scheduled, Delegated, or Eliminated**.
- Use Jira **Filters** to view the most urgent issues.

Using Jira Backlog Features Effectively

1. Rank Issues in the Backlog

Jira allows teams to **drag and drop issues** to manually prioritize tasks.

■ **Best Practice:**

- Place **high-priority bugs and features** at the top.
- Keep backlog **organized by sprint planning cycles**.

---

2. Use Epics to Group Related Work

Epics allow teams to categorize backlog items into high-level initiatives.

■ **Example: Epic - User Management System**

- **Story:** "Allow users to reset passwords"
- **Story:** "Enable two-factor authentication"
- **Task:** "Integrate with Google SSO"

■ **How to Use in Jira:**

- Assign **Epics** to related backlog issues.
- Use the **Epic panel** in the backlog to track progress.

---

3. Create Versions/Releases for Roadmap Planning

Jira allows teams to assign issues to **Versions (Releases)** to organize work based on delivery timelines.

■ **Example: Product Roadmap**

Version	Planned Features
v1.0	User Authentication, Profile Setup
v1.1	Dark Mode, Payment Gateway
v2.0	AI-powered chatbot, Analytics Dashboard

■ **Best Practice:**

- Assign backlog items to **specific versions** to track roadmap progress.

Best Practices for Maintaining a Healthy Backlog

1. Keep the Backlog Clean

■ Regularly **review and remove** outdated issues.
■ Use **JQL filters** to find and close old issues.

Example JQL: Find issues older than 6 months

```
status != Done AND created <= -180d
```

---

2. Balance Feature Development with Bug Fixes

■ Maintain a **40/40/20 rule**:

- **40% Features**
- **40% Bugs and Technical Debt**
- **20% UX and Minor Enhancements**

■ Use **labels like bug, enhancement, tech-debt** to balance sprint work.

---

3. Conduct Backlog Refinement Sessions

■ Hold **weekly backlog grooming sessions**.
■ Ensure backlog issues have:

- **Clear descriptions**
- **Acceptance criteria**
- **Story points or effort estimates**

Conclusion

Prioritizing the Jira backlog **correctly** helps development teams stay focused, deliver high-impact work, and maintain efficiency. By:

✔ Using **MoSCoW, WSJF, and Value vs. Effort techniques** to prioritize work
✔ Leveraging **Jira backlog features** like **ranking, epics, and versions**
✔ Keeping the backlog **clean and structured**
✔ Ensuring backlog refinement is a **continuous process**

…teams can **maximize productivity and ship features faster**.

Streamlining Code Reviews with Jira Integration

Code reviews are an essential part of software development, ensuring **code quality, maintainability, and security**. However, without a structured process, code reviews can become bottlenecks, delaying deployments and increasing technical debt.

By integrating **Jira with code review tools** (such as GitHub, GitLab, or Bitbucket), teams can:

■ **Track pull requests directly in Jira**
■ **Automate issue transitions based on code review status**
■ **Enforce structured review workflows to improve collaboration**

In this chapter, you'll learn:

- **How to integrate Jira with Git repositories for seamless code reviews**
- **Setting up Jira workflows to manage code reviews effectively**
- **Automating status changes based on pull request activity**
- **Best practices for making code reviews efficient**

By the end of this chapter, your team will have a **structured, automated, and efficient** code review process inside Jira.

Understanding Code Review Workflows in Jira

1. The Role of Jira in Code Reviews

Jira helps **track code review progress** by linking development tasks to pull requests (PRs) in **GitHub, GitLab, or Bitbucket**.

A typical Jira-based **code review workflow** looks like this:

To Do → In Progress → Code Review → QA Testing → Done

■ **Jira automatically updates issue status** when a PR is opened, reviewed, or merged.
■ **Reviewers can approve, request changes, or reject code** directly from Jira-linked Git repositories.

2. Benefits of Using Jira for Code Reviews

✔ **Centralized tracking** – All pull requests linked to Jira issues
✔ **Reduced manual work** – PR status automatically updates Jira issues
✔ **Faster code reviews** – Reviewers see assigned PRs directly in Jira
✔ **Stronger collaboration** – Developers, reviewers, and QA teams communicate in one place

---

Integrating Jira with Git Repositories

1. Connecting Jira to GitHub, GitLab, or Bitbucket

Jira integrates natively with Git repositories to **link commits, branches, and pull requests** to Jira issues.

Steps to Integrate Jira with GitHub/GitLab/Bitbucket

1. **Go to Jira Settings → Development Tools**
2. Select **GitHub, GitLab, or Bitbucket**
3. Click **Connect** and authenticate using **OAuth** or **API token**
4. Enable **auto-linking** of pull requests, branches, and commits to Jira issues

■ **Now, Jira will display PR status directly in issues!**

Automating Code Review Workflows in Jira

1. Automatically Move Jira Issues When a PR Is Opened

■ **Use Case:** When a developer opens a **pull request**, the corresponding Jira issue should move to **"Code Review"** automatically.

Jira Automation Rule Setup:

- **Trigger:** Pull Request Created
- **Condition:** Issue Status = "In Progress"
- **Action:** Move issue to **"Code Review"**

JQL Example for Finding PR-Linked Issues:

```
development[pullrequests].open > 0
```

Best Practice: Tag the developer and reviewer in the Jira comment for better visibility.

---

2. Automatically Transition Issues When PRs Are Merged

■ **Use Case:** When a pull request is **merged**, the Jira issue should automatically move to **"Done"** (or "QA Testing" if applicable).

Jira Automation Rule Setup:

- **Trigger:** Pull Request Merged
- **Condition:** Issue Status = "Code Review"
- **Action:** Move issue to **"Done"** or **"QA Testing"**

■ **Bonus:** Add a comment like:

PR merged! Issue {{issue.key}} has been moved to QA Testing.

---

3. Auto-Assign Reviewers Based on Code Ownership

■ **Use Case:** Assign the **code reviewer automatically** based on the affected files (e.g., Frontend Lead for UI changes, Backend Lead for API changes).

Jira Automation Rule Setup:

- **Trigger:** Pull Request Created
- **Condition:** File Path Contains `/backend/` → Assign Backend Lead
- **Action:** Assign issue to appropriate reviewer

■ **JQL for Filtering Backend Issues:**

```
project = "Backend" AND development[pullrequests].open > 0
```

Tracking Code Reviews in Jira

1. Using Jira Dashboards for Code Review Metrics

Jira **dashboards** help track code review progress with widgets like:

Widget Name	Purpose
Pull Requests Awaiting Review	Shows all PRs that need attention
Average Review Time	Tracks how long reviews take
Code Review Backlog	Displays issues stuck in the "Code Review" stage

2. Using JQL for Code Review Reports

■ **Find all issues currently in "Code Review"**

```
status = "Code Review" AND development[pullrequests].open > 0
```

■ **Find PRs waiting for review for more than 3 days**

```
status = "Code Review" AND updated <= -3d
```

■ **Track unresolved issues with PRs merged but not closed**

```
status != Done AND development[pullrequests].merged > 0
```

Tip: Add these JQL queries to Jira **custom dashboards** for better visibility.

Best Practices for Efficient Code Reviews

1. Enforce Code Review SLAs (Service Level Agreements)

■ **Set a rule that PRs must be reviewed within 24 hours**
■ Use Jira Automation to **remind reviewers** after 24 hours

2. Link Jira Issues to PRs Using Smart Branch Naming

■ Use **Jira issue keys in branch names** (e.g., `feature/JIRA-123-authentication`)
■ This ensures PRs are **automatically linked** to Jira issues

3. Use Labels to Categorize Code Reviews

■ Label PRs as **urgent-review**, **security-review**, or **standard-review**
■ Create Jira filters to prioritize urgent reviews

Example JQL for Urgent Code Reviews:

```
status = "Code Review" AND labels IN ("urgent-review")
```

---

4. Encourage Collaborative Reviews in Jira Comments

■ Use **Jira comments for discussion** instead of Slack/email
■ Tag relevant team members in review-related updates

---

5. Automate Deployment After Code Review Approval

■ Trigger **CI/CD pipelines** from Jira when code reviews are approved
■ Use Jira automation to **transition issues to "Ready for Deployment"**

■ **Example Automation Rule:**

- **Trigger:** Pull Request Approved
- **Action:** Move Jira issue to **"Ready for Deployment"**

Best Practice: Use Jira DevOps Integration to auto-trigger deployments after successful reviews.

Conclusion

By integrating **Jira with Git repositories and automating code review workflows**, teams can:

✔ **Track pull requests inside Jira** for full visibility
✔ **Auto-transition issues based on PR activity**
✔ **Assign reviewers automatically** to reduce delays
✔ **Monitor code review SLAs with JQL and dashboards**

A **structured, automated code review process** improves collaboration, speeds up development, and enhances **code quality**.

Managing Dependencies Between Tasks and Teams

In modern software development, different teams—**frontend, backend, DevOps, QA, and product management**—must collaborate efficiently. However, without a structured approach, **task dependencies** can create bottlenecks, causing delays and misalignment between teams.

Jira provides **robust tools** to manage task dependencies, ensuring that teams can:

■ **Visualize and track dependencies** between tasks and teams
■ **Automatically enforce dependency rules** in workflows
■ **Prevent blockers from halting development**
■ **Use Jira reports to identify dependency risks early**

In this chapter, you'll learn:

- **Types of task dependencies in software development**
- **How to link related Jira issues effectively**
- **Using dependency management reports and visualizations**
- **Automating dependency tracking for efficiency**

By the end of this chapter, you'll be able to **manage cross-team dependencies** efficiently, improving collaboration and project flow.

Understanding Task Dependencies in Jira

1. Types of Task Dependencies

Software development teams often face **four types of dependencies**:

Dependency Type	Description	Example
Finish-to-Start (F-S)	Task A must finish before Task B starts	"Backend API must be ready before frontend UI development begins"
Start-to-Start (S-S)	Task A and Task B must start together	"QA testing begins when developers start integration testing"
Finish-to-Finish (F-F)	Task A and Task B must finish together	"Frontend and backend features must be ready for deployment simultaneously"
Start-to-Finish (S-F)	Task B cannot finish until Task A starts	"Production migration cannot finish until server configuration begins"

■ **Best Practice:** Identify dependencies **early** in sprint planning to avoid last-minute blockers.

Linking Dependent Issues in Jira

Jira provides **built-in issue linking** to track dependencies between tasks.

1. Using Issue Links to Track Dependencies

Jira allows you to link tasks with predefined **link types** such as:

- **"Blocks"** → Used when Task A prevents Task B from progressing
- **"Is Blocked By"** → The inverse of "Blocks"
- **"Relates To"** → Used for tasks that are connected but not strictly dependent
- **"Depends On"** → Used when one task must be completed before another starts

Steps to Link Issues in Jira

1. Open a **Jira issue**
2. Scroll to the **Issue Links** section
3. Click **"Link Issue"**
4. Select the appropriate **link type** (e.g., "Blocks," "Is Blocked By")
5. Choose the related issue
6. Click **Save**

■ **Now, teams can track issue dependencies directly from Jira!**

2. Using Epics to Organize Cross-Team Dependencies

Epics allow teams to **group related tasks** under a single high-level goal.

■ **Example Epic: "User Authentication System"**

- **Backend Task:** "Implement OAuth login API"
- **Frontend Task:** "Build UI for login page"
- **QA Task:** "Test login authentication flow"

Best Practice: Use Epics for cross-team features to ensure aligned execution.

Visualizing Dependencies with Jira Reports

1. Using the Dependency Map in Advanced Roadmaps

Jira Advanced Roadmaps provide a **Dependency Map** to visualize task relationships.

Steps to Access Dependency Map:

1. Go to **Plans** → **Advanced Roadmaps**
2. Select your Jira project
3. Click **"View Dependencies"**
4. Use the **graph view** to identify dependency risks

■ **Now, teams can see all task dependencies at a glance!**

2. Using Jira Filters to Identify Blocked Issues

Jira Query Language (**JQL**) can be used to find tasks **blocked by dependencies**.

■ **Find all blocked issues:**

```
issueLinkType = "is blocked by"
```

■ **Find issues waiting for API completion:**

```
issueLinkType = "depends on" AND summary ~ "API"
```

■ **Find overdue dependent tasks:**

```
issueLinkType = "blocks" AND dueDate < now()
```

Tip: Save these JQL filters as **custom dashboards** to track dependencies in real-time.

Automating Dependency Tracking in Jira

1. Auto-Transitioning Issues Based on Dependencies

■ **Use Case:** When a blocking task is completed, automatically transition dependent tasks.

Jira Automation Rule Setup:

- **Trigger:** Issue Status Changed → "Done"
- **Condition:** Linked Issue Exists with "Is Blocked By"
- **Action:** Transition the blocked issue to "In Progress"

■ **Now, developers don't have to manually update dependencies!**

---

2. Sending Alerts for Unresolved Dependencies

■ **Use Case:** If a dependent issue is not resolved within **3 days**, notify the team.

Jira Automation Rule Setup:

- **Trigger:** Scheduled (Daily)
- **Condition:** Linked Issue Still in "To Do" After 3 Days
- **Action:** Send Email to Assignee & Slack Notification

■ **Now, teams get proactive alerts to resolve blockers!**

Best Practices for Managing Dependencies

1. Identify Dependencies During Sprint Planning

■ Before starting a sprint, check for **unfinished dependencies**.
■ Use Jira's **Advanced Roadmaps** to visualize interdependencies.

2. Use Labels to Track Dependency Categories

■ Label issues as **"critical-dependency"**, **"cross-team"**, or **"backend-blocker"**.
■ Create Jira filters to **prioritize dependent issues**.

Example JQL for Critical Dependencies:

```
labels IN ("critical-dependency")
```

3. Encourage Communication Between Teams

■ Developers, QA, and DevOps should **collaborate on dependent tasks**.
■ Use **Jira comments** and **Slack notifications** for real-time updates.

4. Regularly Review and Close Old Dependencies

■ Use JQL to **find unresolved dependencies older than 30 days**.
■ If dependencies are outdated, **archive or remove** them.

■ **Example JQL for Old Dependencies:**

```
issueLinkType = "is blocked by" AND updated <= -30d
```

Conclusion

Effectively managing dependencies in Jira helps teams:

✔ **Track blockers and prevent bottlenecks**
✔ **Ensure smooth handoffs between teams**
✔ **Use automation to transition tasks and send alerts**
✔ **Leverage dashboards and JQL filters for proactive management**

By implementing **issue linking, automation, and dependency reports**, your team will reduce delays and ensure efficient **cross-team collaboration**.

Handling Bugs and Hotfixes in Jira

Bugs are inevitable in software development, but **efficient bug tracking and resolution workflows** can minimize their impact. Jira provides **powerful tools** for logging, prioritizing, and resolving bugs while managing **urgent hotfixes** efficiently.

By implementing a structured approach, development teams can:

■ **Quickly triage and prioritize bugs**
■ **Streamline hotfix workflows for critical issues**
■ **Automate bug tracking with integrations and reporting**
■ **Ensure bugs do not get lost in the backlog**

In this chapter, you'll learn:

- **How to set up bug tracking workflows in Jira**
- **Best practices for managing hotfixes**
- **Using JQL filters to monitor bug trends**
- **Automating bug tracking for better efficiency**

By the end of this chapter, your team will have a **clear, structured process** for handling bugs and deploying hotfixes efficiently.

Setting Up a Bug Tracking Workflow in Jira

1. Creating a Bug Issue Type

Jira allows teams to classify defects using the **"Bug" issue type**, separate from feature development.

■ **Default Bug Workflow:**

Reported → To Do → In Progress → In Review → QA Testing → Done

2. Defining Bug Severity and Priority

To ensure **high-impact bugs get resolved first**, use **Severity** and **Priority** fields.

Field	Purpose	Examples
Severity	Measures the bug's technical impact	Critical, Major, Minor, Trivial
Priority	Measures urgency based on business impact	Blocker, High, Medium, Low

■ **Best Practice:**

- Critical **bugs with Blocker priority** → Immediate hotfix
- Major **bugs with High priority** → Addressed in the next sprint
- Minor **bugs with Low priority** → Scheduled for later

Logging Bugs in Jira

1. Creating a Bug Report Template

A well-structured bug report helps developers **quickly reproduce and fix issues**.

Bug Report Format in Jira

Field	Example
Summary	"Login Page Crashes on Safari"
Description	"Users see a blank screen when logging in on Safari 15. Bug not present in Chrome or Firefox."
Steps to Reproduce	1. Open Safari 15, 2. Go to /login, 3. Enter valid credentials, 4. Click "Login"
Expected Behavior	"User should be redirected to the dashboard"
Actual Behavior	"Blank screen appears"
Severity	Critical
Priority	Blocker
Environment	MacOS 12, Safari 15.0
Attachments	Screenshot, Logs, Video Recording

■ **Best Practice:** Use **Jira Custom Fields** to enforce structured bug reporting.

Managing Hotfixes Efficiently

Hotfixes are **urgent bug fixes** that need **immediate deployment outside regular releases**.

1. Hotfix Workflow in Jira

To separate hotfixes from regular bugs, use a dedicated **Hotfix Workflow**:

Reported → In Progress → Code Review → Staging → Production → Done

2. Creating a "Hotfix" Label or Issue Type

■ Add a **"hotfix" label** or create a **"Hotfix" issue type** for urgent bug fixes.

Example JQL to Find Open Hotfixes

```
issuetype = "Hotfix" AND status != Done ORDER BY priority DESC
```

3. Auto-Assigning Hotfixes to Senior Developers

■ **Jira Automation Rule:**

- **Trigger:** Issue Type = "Hotfix"

- **Condition:** Priority = Blocker or High
- **Action:** Auto-assign to the **Senior Developer or Tech Lead**

Best Practice: Use Jira's **Workflow Conditions** to **restrict hotfix approvals to senior engineers**.

Automating Bug Tracking with Jira

1. Auto-Linking Bugs to Features

■ If a bug is reported during feature development, link it to the related **Story** or **Epic**.

Example Jira Automation Rule:

- **Trigger:** Bug Created
- **Condition:** Summary Contains "Login"
- **Action:** Link Bug to **Epic: Authentication System**

■ Now, all login-related bugs are grouped under the authentication feature!

---

2. Sending Slack Alerts for High-Priority Bugs

■ Jira Automation Rule:

- **Trigger:** Bug Created with Priority = Blocker
- **Action:** Send Slack Notification to #dev-alerts

Example Slack Message:

🔔 Critical Bug Alert: "Login Page Crash" (JIRA-456)
Severity: Critical | Priority: Blocker
Assigned to: @JohnDoe

■ Now, teams get instant alerts for critical issues!

---

3. Escalating Unresolved Bugs Automatically

■ Jira Automation Rule:

- **Trigger:** Bug is **open for more than 7 days**
- **Condition:** Priority = High
- **Action:** Send Email to Engineering Manager

JQL Query for Escalation:

```
issuetype = Bug AND priority = High AND status != Done AND updated <= -7d
```

■ Now, long-standing critical bugs are automatically escalated!

Monitoring Bug Trends with Jira Reports

1. Creating a Bug Tracking Dashboard

Key Metrics to Track in Jira Dashboards:

Report	Purpose
Open vs. Resolved Bugs	Monitor bug resolution efficiency
Bugs by Priority	Ensure high-priority bugs get addressed first
Bug Resolution Time	Track average time to fix issues
Hotfix Deployment Success Rate	Ensure hotfixes are effective and stable

Best Practice: Set up **weekly automated reports** to monitor bug resolution progress.

---

2. Using JQL for Bug Reports

Find all open critical bugs:

```
issuetype = Bug AND priority = Blocker AND status != Done
```

Find all bugs reported in the last 30 days:

```
issuetype = Bug AND created >= -30d
```

Track bugs by component (e.g., Authentication, Checkout, API):

```
issuetype = Bug AND component = "Authentication"
```

Tip: Use these JQL queries in Jira dashboards to **monitor trends in bug tracking**.

Best Practices for Handling Bugs in Jira

1. Triage and Prioritize Bugs Immediately

- Set up **daily or weekly bug triage meetings**.
- Use Jira **automation to auto-assign critical bugs**.

2. Separate Hotfixes from Regular Bug Fixes

- Use a **dedicated "Hotfix" issue type or label**.
- Track hotfixes separately from feature development.

3. Automate Bug Tracking and Escalations

- Use **Jira automation** to notify teams of unresolved issues.
- Escalate **long-standing critical bugs** to engineering leads.

4. Continuously Monitor and Improve Bug Resolution Rates

- Track bug resolution metrics using **Jira dashboards**.
- Set SLAs for bug resolution based on **severity and priority**.

Conclusion

A **structured bug and hotfix management workflow in Jira** ensures that:

✔ **Critical bugs are addressed quickly** with priority-based tracking
✔ **Hotfixes are deployed efficiently** using automation
✔ **Jira dashboards provide real-time bug tracking insights**
✔ **Teams maintain a proactive approach to bug resolution**

By leveraging **Jira's issue tracking, automation, and reporting**, your team can **improve software quality and reduce downtime** effectively.

Reporting: Burndown Charts, Velocity, and Cycle Time

Effective software development isn't just about **completing tasks**—it's also about **measuring progress and optimizing workflows**. Jira offers powerful **reporting tools** that help teams track sprint performance, identify bottlenecks, and improve delivery predictability.

In this chapter, you'll learn:

■ **How to use Burndown Charts to track sprint progress**
■ **How to measure development speed with Velocity Reports**
■ **How to analyze Cycle Time to improve efficiency**
■ **Best practices for interpreting and acting on these reports**

By the end of this chapter, your team will be able to **leverage Jira's reporting tools to improve planning, execution, and delivery**.

Understanding Key Agile Metrics

1. What Are Agile Metrics?

Agile teams rely on **quantitative metrics** to track progress, efficiency, and performance. The three most important metrics in Jira are:

Metric	Purpose	Best For
Burndown Chart	Tracks sprint progress	Scrum teams
Velocity Report	Measures work completed per sprint	Predicting team capacity
Cycle Time	Measures time from task creation to completion	Kanban and DevOps teams

■ **Best Practice:** Use these reports **together** for a complete view of team performance.

Using Burndown Charts in Jira

1. What Is a Burndown Chart?

A **Burndown Chart** tracks the progress of a sprint by showing:

- **Remaining work** (story points, tasks, or hours)
- **Expected progress vs. actual progress**
- **Scope creep (if new work is added mid-sprint)**

2. How to Access the Burndown Chart in Jira

1. Navigate to **Jira → Reports → Burndown Chart**
2. Select your **Sprint** from the dropdown

3. Analyze the **graph** to track remaining work

3. How to Read a Burndown Chart

■ **Ideal Burndown:** A smooth, downward slope reaching **zero work remaining** by sprint end.
■ **Scope Creep:** A sudden **increase in work** during the sprint.
■ **Slow Progress:** A **flat line** indicating work is not being completed as expected.

Example Burndown Chart Analysis:

Observation	Meaning	Solution
Work is not decreasing	Tasks are not being completed	Investigate blockers
Work suddenly increases	New work was added mid-sprint	Lock sprint backlog after planning
Work finishes too early	Sprint was under-planned	Increase sprint workload in future iterations

■ **Best Practice:** Review the **Burndown Chart** in Sprint Retrospectives to identify trends and improve planning.

Measuring Team Velocity with Jira

1. What Is Velocity?

Velocity measures how much work a team completes per sprint, helping teams **predict future capacity**.

🔦 **Formula:**

Velocity = Total Story Points Completed / Number of Sprints

2. How to Access the Velocity Report in Jira

1. Navigate to **Jira → Reports → Velocity Chart**
2. Select your **Scrum board**
3. Analyze the chart for **average work completed per sprint**

3. How to Use the Velocity Report for Sprint Planning

Scenario	What It Means	Sprint Planning Action
Velocity is stable	Team is predictable	Use average velocity for planning
Velocity is increasing	Team is improving efficiency	Increase sprint scope gradually
Velocity is fluctuating	Team has inconsistent workload	Investigate blockers and work balance

■ **Best Practice:** Use the **last 3-5 sprints** to calculate an **average velocity** for planning future sprints.

Analyzing Cycle Time in Jira

1. What Is Cycle Time?

Cycle Time measures the **total time taken** from **task creation to completion**. It's crucial for **Kanban teams** and **DevOps workflows**.

🔦 Formula:

Cycle Time = Task Completion Date - Task Creation Date

2. How to Access Cycle Time in Jira

1. Navigate to **Jira → Reports → Control Chart**
2. Select your **Kanban or Scrum board**
3. Analyze the **Cycle Time trend**

3. How to Use Cycle Time to Improve Efficiency

Cycle Time Pattern	What It Means	Action Required
Short & Consistent	Tasks are flowing smoothly	Maintain current workflow
Long & Increasing	Work is taking too long	Identify bottlenecks
Highly Variable	Some tasks take too long	Investigate blockers and work complexity

⬛ **Best Practice:** Identify **tasks with high Cycle Time** using JQL and optimize the workflow.

Example JQL Query to Find Slow Tasks

```
status = Done AND updated >= -30d ORDER BY resolutiondate ASC
```

Automating Jira Reports for Better Insights

1. Automate Weekly Burndown Reports

⬛ **Jira Automation Rule:**

- **Trigger:** Sprint End
- **Action:** Send Burndown Chart via email to the team

2. Notify the Team When Velocity Drops

⬛ **Jira Automation Rule:**

- **Trigger:** Sprint Completed
- **Condition:** Velocity is **lower than the last 3 sprints**
- **Action:** Send Slack message:

  🔔 Sprint velocity dropped! Review blockers in Sprint Retrospective.

3. Alert Teams on High Cycle Time Tasks

■ **Jira Automation Rule:**

- **Trigger:** Issue remains in "In Progress" for **>10 days**
- **Action:** Notify Developer Lead:

  ▲ Issue JIRA-456 has been in "In Progress" for 10+ days. Review for blockers!

Best Practices for Using Jira Reports

■ 1. Review Reports in Sprint Retrospectives

- Discuss **Burndown trends** and **Sprint velocity**.
- Identify blockers using **Cycle Time reports**.

■ 2. Compare Reports Across Multiple Sprints

- Use a **3-sprint average** to **avoid anomalies** in velocity trends.
- Track **long-term improvements** with Burndown trends.

■ 3. Integrate Reports with Stakeholder Updates

- Share **Velocity Reports with product owners**.
- Use **Burndown Charts in sprint reviews** for transparency.

■ 4. Keep Reports Simple and Actionable

- Focus on **one or two insights per report**.
- Use **automation to highlight key trends** instead of overwhelming data.

Conclusion

Jira's reporting tools help teams:

✔ **Track sprint progress with Burndown Charts**
✔ **Measure and predict workload using Velocity Reports**
✔ **Optimize workflows by analyzing Cycle Time**
✔ **Automate reporting for better decision-making**

By leveraging **Jira's built-in reports and automation**, teams can continuously improve sprint execution, deliver more predictably, and reduce workflow inefficiencies.

Part 5:
Integrations and Extensions

Connecting Jira to CI/CD Pipelines (Jenkins, GitHub Actions)

Continuous Integration and Continuous Deployment (**CI/CD**) pipelines streamline software delivery by automating **builds, testing, and deployments**. When integrated with Jira, CI/CD tools such as **Jenkins, GitHub Actions, and GitLab CI/CD** provide real-time visibility into development progress, ensuring that Jira issues reflect the latest code status.

By integrating Jira with CI/CD pipelines, teams can:

■ **Automatically update Jira issues based on CI/CD events**
■ **Trigger builds directly from Jira**
■ **Track deployment status within Jira issues**
■ **Reduce manual handoffs and improve traceability**

In this chapter, you'll learn:

- **How CI/CD pipelines work with Jira**
- **Setting up Jira integration with Jenkins and GitHub Actions**
- **Automating issue tracking with deployment statuses**
- **Best practices for integrating Jira with CI/CD workflows**

By the end of this chapter, your team will be able to **connect Jira with CI/CD tools**, automating workflow updates and improving development efficiency.

Understanding CI/CD Integration with Jira

1. Why Integrate Jira with CI/CD?

Without CI/CD integration, Jira issues often require **manual status updates**. Developers might forget to update issue statuses when code is merged or deployed, leading to **misalignment between development and project tracking**.

By integrating Jira with **Jenkins, GitHub Actions, or GitLab CI/CD**, teams can:

- **Auto-update Jira issues** when a pull request is merged
- **Track deployment history** within Jira
- **View build results and logs directly in Jira**
- **Ensure compliance by linking Jira issues to builds**

■ **Best Practice:** Use Jira integration to create a **single source of truth** for tracking development progress.

Setting Up Jira Integration with Jenkins

1. Installing the Jira Plugin for Jenkins

Jenkins provides a **Jira Plugin** that allows automatic updates between **Jenkins builds** and **Jira issues**.

Steps to Install the Jira Plugin in Jenkins:

1. Navigate to **Jenkins Dashboard → Manage Jenkins → Manage Plugins**
2. Search for **"Jira Plugin"**
3. Click **Install** and restart Jenkins

■ **Now, Jenkins can interact with Jira to update issues automatically!**

---

2. Connecting Jenkins to Jira

After installing the plugin, configure Jenkins to communicate with Jira.

Steps to Configure Jira in Jenkins:

1. Go to **Jenkins Dashboard → Manage Jenkins → Configure System**
2. Scroll to **Jira Integration**
3. Enter your **Jira Base URL** (e.g., `https://yourcompany.atlassian.net`)
4. Add **Jira API Token Authentication**
5. Click **Test Connection** to verify

■ **Now, Jenkins can access Jira for automation!**

---

3. Automatically Updating Jira Issues from Jenkins

Use Jenkins to **update Jira issue statuses based on build success or failure**.

Example: Updating Jira When a Build Passes

1. Open your **Jenkins job**
2. Click **Post-build Actions → Update Jira Issue**
3. Select **"Change issue status"**
4. Choose **"Done"** if the build is successful
5. Save the job

■ **Now, Jira issues automatically move to "Done" after a successful Jenkins build!**

Jira Comment Example After a Successful Build:
■ Build #45 for JIRA-123 has passed! View logs: [Jenkins Build Link]

Setting Up Jira Integration with GitHub Actions

GitHub Actions provides a **built-in CI/CD pipeline** that can be linked to Jira.

1. Generating a Jira API Token

Before integrating GitHub Actions with Jira, generate an **API token** for authentication.

Steps to Generate Jira API Token:

1. Go to **Jira → Account Settings → Security**
2. Click **Create API Token**
3. Copy the token and store it securely

---

2. Adding Jira API Token to GitHub Secrets

1. Go to your **GitHub repository → Settings → Secrets and Variables → Actions**
2. Click **New Repository Secret**
3. Name it **JIRA_API_TOKEN**
4. Paste the **Jira API Token**

■ Now, GitHub Actions can authenticate with Jira!

---

3. Automating Jira Issue Updates from GitHub Actions

Use a **GitHub Actions workflow** to update Jira when a PR is merged.

Example GitHub Actions Workflow:

```
name: Update Jira on PR Merge
on:
  pull_request:
    types:
      - closed

jobs:
  update-jira:
    runs-on: ubuntu-latest
    steps:
      - name: Update Jira Issue
        run: |
          curl -X POST -u "your-email:${{ secrets.JIRA_API_TOKEN }}" \
          -H "Content-Type: application/json" \
          --data '{
            "fields": {
              "status": "Done"
            }
          }' \
          "https://yourcompany.atlassian.net/rest/api/2/issue/JIRA-123/transitions"
```

■ Now, Jira automatically updates when a PR is merged!

Jira Comment Example After PR Merge:
■ Pull Request Merged! Issue JIRA-123 is now marked as "Done".

Automating Deployment Tracking in Jira

1. Linking Jira Issues to CI/CD Deployments

To track deployments, link Jira issues to deployment events in **Jenkins or GitHub Actions**.

■ **Best Practice:** Use **Jira Smart Commits** in Git messages.

Example Commit Message with Jira Smart Commit:

Fixing login bug [JIRA-456] #close

■ **This automatically updates Jira issue JIRA-456 to "Done" when merged!**

---

2. Using Jira Deployment Tracking Dashboard

Jira provides a **Deployment Tracking View** to monitor software releases.

How to Enable Deployment Tracking in Jira:

1. Go to **Jira → Apps → Deployment Tracking**
2. Connect your **CI/CD tool (Jenkins, GitHub Actions, Bitbucket Pipelines, etc.)**
3. View real-time **deployment status** in Jira

■ **Now, teams can see which Jira issues are deployed in each environment!**

Best Practices for CI/CD Integration with Jira

■ 1. Use Jira Smart Commits for Automatic Updates

- Add #close or #done in Git commit messages to **auto-close Jira issues**.
- Example:

Implemented new authentication flow [JIRA-789] #done

■ 2. Set Up Notifications for Failed Builds

- Use Jira Automation to notify the team if a **Jenkins or GitHub Actions build fails**.
- Example Rule:
  - **Trigger:** Jenkins build fails
  - **Action:** Send Jira comment:

    ▲ Build #57 failed! Jira issue JIRA-123 requires attention.

■ 3. Track All Deployments in Jira

- Enable **Deployment Tracking** to monitor where each Jira issue is deployed.
- Create a Jira dashboard showing **which issues are in production**.

Conclusion

Integrating Jira with **CI/CD pipelines** using **Jenkins or GitHub Actions** ensures:

✔ **Automated Jira issue updates** when PRs are merged or builds pass
✔ **Seamless tracking of deployments** in Jira
✔ **Better visibility into development progress** for the entire team
✔ **Faster feedback loops** and reduced manual updates

By connecting **Jira with your CI/CD pipeline**, your team can automate workflow updates, improve traceability, and ensure smoother software delivery.

Syncing Jira with Version Control (GitHub, GitLab, Bitbucket)

For software development teams, **Jira and version control systems (VCS)** such as **GitHub, GitLab, and Bitbucket** go hand in hand. Without proper integration, tracking code changes and linking them to Jira issues becomes a manual and error-prone process.

By integrating Jira with **Git repositories**, teams can:

■ **Automatically link commits, branches, and pull requests (PRs) to Jira issues**
■ **Track development progress without switching between Jira and Git**
■ **Improve visibility into feature development, bug fixes, and hotfixes**
■ **Streamline collaboration between developers and project managers**

In this chapter, you'll learn:

- **Why syncing Jira with version control is important**
- **How to integrate Jira with GitHub, GitLab, and Bitbucket**
- **Best practices for using Jira Smart Commits to automate updates**
- **How to track code changes directly from Jira**

By the end of this chapter, your team will be able to **fully integrate Jira with Git repositories, improving workflow automation and traceability**.

Why Sync Jira with Version Control?

Tracking **code changes and Jira issues separately** can lead to:

✘ **Developers forgetting to update Jira issues after a commit**
✘ **Project managers lacking visibility into which features are under development**
✘ **Bug fixes and hotfixes getting lost in unlinked commits**

By syncing Jira with Git repositories, teams can:

✔ **See commits, branches, and pull requests inside Jira issues**
✔ **Automatically transition Jira issues based on Git activity**
✔ **Improve release tracking by linking Jira issues to deployments**

■ **Best Practice: Use Jira as a single source of truth** by linking development work directly to tasks.

Integrating Jira with GitHub

1. Setting Up Jira-GitHub Integration

To connect Jira with **GitHub**, use **Atlassian's GitHub Integration for Jira**.

Steps to Integrate GitHub with Jira:

1. Go to **Jira → Apps → Find new apps**
2. Search for **"GitHub for Jira"**

3. Click **Install and Configure**
4. Authenticate with **your GitHub account**
5. Select **GitHub repositories** to connect with Jira
6. Enable **auto-linking of commits, branches, and pull requests**

■ Now, GitHub activity will be visible in Jira issues!

---

2. Using Jira Smart Commits in GitHub

Jira **Smart Commits** allow developers to **update Jira issues directly from commit messages**.

Example Smart Commit Syntax in GitHub:
git commit -m "Fixed login bug [JIRA-123] #done"

Smart Commit Action	Description	Example
#done	Marks the Jira issue as completed	Fix navbar issue [JIRA-456] #done
#in-progress	Moves the issue to "In Progress"	Started API refactor [JIRA-789] #in-progress
#comment	Adds a comment to the issue	Refactored function [JIRA-101] #comment Code optimized

■ **Best Practice:** Encourage developers to **include Jira issue keys in commit messages** for automatic linking.

Integrating Jira with GitLab

1. Setting Up Jira-GitLab Integration

For **GitLab**, Jira integration is available as a **built-in feature**.

Steps to Connect GitLab with Jira:

1. Go to **GitLab → Project Settings → Integrations**
2. Search for **"Jira"** and click **Enable**
3. Enter your **Jira Base URL** (https://yourcompany.atlassian.net)
4. Add **Jira API Token Authentication**
5. Save the settings

■ Now, GitLab merge requests and commits will appear in Jira!

---

2. Auto-Updating Jira Issues from GitLab

Use **GitLab's commit message automation** to trigger Jira updates.

Example Smart Commit in GitLab:

git commit -m "Updated README [JIRA-987] #review"

GitLab Smart Commit	Jira Update
#done	Moves Jira issue to **Done**
#review	Moves Jira issue to **In Review**
#fix	Marks issue as **Bug Fixed**

■ **Best Practice:** Use **merge request descriptions** to reference Jira issues.

Example GitLab Merge Request Description:

Fixes JIRA-234: Resolves database connection issue.

Integrating Jira with Bitbucket

1. Setting Up Jira-Bitbucket Integration

Since Bitbucket is an **Atlassian product**, integration with Jira is seamless.

Steps to Connect Bitbucket with Jira:

1. Go to **Jira → Apps → Bitbucket Integration**
2. Click **"Connect Bitbucket"**
3. Authenticate using **your Bitbucket credentials**
4. Select **repositories** to sync with Jira

■ **Now, Bitbucket activity is tracked inside Jira!**

---

2. Automating Jira Issue Updates from Bitbucket

Bitbucket **automatically links commits and pull requests to Jira** if the issue key is included in the commit message.

Example Commit Message in Bitbucket:

git commit -m "Implemented user registration [JIRA-567] #done"

Example Bitbucket Pull Request Title:

Fix payment processing error [JIRA-678]

■ **Now, Jira issues get updated automatically when PRs are merged!**

Viewing Git Commits and PRs Inside Jira

1. Using the "Development" Panel in Jira Issues

Once version control is integrated, Jira displays a **Development Panel** inside each issue.

This panel shows:

✔ **Branches linked to the issue**
✔ **Commits referencing the issue**
✔ **Pull Requests associated with the issue**
✔ **Deployment history**

■ **Best Practice:** Encourage developers to **check Jira issues for related Git activity** before starting work.

Automating Version Control Workflows with Jira

1. Automatically Transition Jira Issues Based on Git Activity

Use **Jira Automation** to move issues based on **commit or pull request events**.

Example Jira Automation Rule:

- **Trigger:** A **pull request is merged**
- **Condition:** The linked issue is **"In Review"**
- **Action:** Move issue to **"Done"**

■ **Now, Jira issues update automatically when PRs are merged!**

---

2. Sending Slack Alerts for Code Changes

Use **Jira Automation + Slack** to notify teams when important code changes occur.

Example Jira Automation Rule:

- **Trigger:** A **new commit references a Jira issue**
- **Action:** Send Slack notification:

  🔔 New Commit Linked to JIRA-456!
  View Changes: [GitHub Commit Link]

■ **Now, teams stay updated on code changes in real-time!**

Best Practices for Syncing Jira with Version Control

■ 1. Always Include Jira Issue Keys in Commits

- Use [JIRA-123] in commit messages to **auto-link code changes**.

■ 2. Use Jira Smart Commits for Automation

- Use #done, #review, or #comment to update issues **without opening Jira**.

■ 3. Track Pull Request Status in Jira

- Ensure **PRs are linked to Jira issues** for better visibility.

■ 4. Enable Deployment Tracking in Jira

- Use the **Jira Deployment Panel** to see which issues are in **staging or production**.

Conclusion

By integrating **Jira with GitHub, GitLab, or Bitbucket**, teams can:

✔ **Track development work inside Jira without switching tools**
✔ **Automatically update Jira issues from commit messages**
✔ **Improve visibility into code changes and deployments**
✔ **Streamline collaboration between developers and project managers**

In the next chapter, we'll explore **Extending Jira with Marketplace Apps (ScriptRunner, Zephyr)** to further enhance Jira's capabilities.

Extending Jira with Marketplace Apps (ScriptRunner, Zephyr)

Jira is a powerful tool on its own, but for **complex development workflows, automation, and test management**, teams often require **additional functionality**. Atlassian's **Marketplace Apps**, such as **ScriptRunner** and **Zephyr**, enable teams to **customize Jira**, automate tasks, and integrate advanced testing capabilities.

By leveraging **Jira Marketplace Apps**, teams can:

■ **Automate repetitive Jira tasks with ScriptRunner**
■ **Enhance test management with Zephyr**
■ **Extend Jira's capabilities without complex coding**
■ **Integrate custom workflows, scripts, and reports**

In this chapter, you'll learn:

- **Why extending Jira with apps is beneficial**
- **How to use ScriptRunner for automation and scripting**
- **How to manage test cases efficiently with Zephyr**
- **Best practices for selecting and implementing Jira Marketplace apps**

By the end of this chapter, you'll know how to **enhance Jira's functionality** to better suit your development team's needs.

Why Extend Jira with Marketplace Apps?

Jira's **out-of-the-box features** cover most Agile development needs, but certain teams may require **advanced automation, scripting, or test management**.

Key reasons to extend Jira:

✔ **Automate complex workflows** (e.g., bulk issue updates, auto-assigning tasks)
✔ **Enhance reporting** with custom JQL scripts and dashboards
✔ **Improve test case management** by integrating test execution inside Jira
✔ **Integrate external tools** (e.g., CI/CD, security testing, custom integrations)

■ **Best Practice:** Evaluate apps based on your team's **specific requirements** and avoid unnecessary overhead.

Automating Jira with ScriptRunner

1. What Is ScriptRunner?

ScriptRunner is a **powerful Jira app** that allows teams to:

- **Automate workflows and issue transitions**
- **Execute bulk updates on issues**
- **Extend JQL functionality** for advanced reporting
- **Write custom scripts using Groovy**

■ **Best For:** Development teams that want to **customize and automate Jira** without waiting for Atlassian updates.

---

2. Key Features of ScriptRunner

A. Automating Issue Workflows

ScriptRunner allows you to **auto-transition Jira issues** based on events such as:

■ **Automatically move an issue to "In Progress" when development starts**
■ **Reopen a bug if a test case fails**
■ **Close all subtasks when a parent issue is completed**

Example ScriptRunner Automation: Auto-Assign Issues Based on Components

```
import com.atlassian.jira.component.ComponentAccessor

def issue = event.issue
def componentManager = ComponentAccessor.getComponentManager()
def userManager = ComponentAccessor.getUserManager()

def components = issue.getComponents()
if (components) {
    def assignedUser = userManager.getUserByName(components[0].getName())
    issue.setAssignee(assignedUser)
}
```

■ **Now, Jira will auto-assign issues based on the selected component!**

B. Enhancing JQL for Advanced Searches

By default, Jira Query Language (**JQL**) has limitations. **ScriptRunner extends JQL** to:

+ **Find all issues where the last comment was made by a specific user**
+ **Search for issues with long resolution times**
+ **Identify issues where no updates have been made in the last 30 days**

Example: Find Issues Stuck in "In Progress" for More Than 10 Days

```
issueFunction in dateCompare("", "updated +10d < now()") AND status = "In Progress"
```

■ **This helps teams track delayed tasks easily!**

C. Running Bulk Updates on Jira Issues

Managing large-scale issue updates manually can be tedious. **ScriptRunner lets you update issues in bulk** with automation.

■ **Example:** Close all Jira issues linked to a specific release version

```
def version = ComponentAccessor.getVersionManager().getVersion("ProjectKey",
"1.2.0")
def issues = ComponentAccessor.getIssueManager().getIssuesByFixVersion(version)

issues.each { issue ->
    issue.setStatus("Done")
}
```

■ Now, all issues linked to version 1.2.0 are automatically closed!

Managing Test Cases in Jira with Zephyr

1. What Is Zephyr?

Zephyr is a **test management solution** that integrates **directly inside Jira**, allowing teams to:

* **Create, manage, and execute test cases** inside Jira
* **Link test cases to development tasks and bug reports**
* **Generate test execution reports and analytics**
* **Automate testing workflows with CI/CD pipelines**

■ Best For: QA teams that want **test case tracking inside Jira without an external tool**.

---

2. Setting Up Zephyr in Jira

A. Installing Zephyr

1. Go to **Jira → Apps → Find new apps**
2. Search for **"Zephyr Scale" or "Zephyr Squad"**
3. Click **Install and Configure**
4. Add Zephyr to your Jira project

■ Now, test management is integrated inside Jira!

---

3. Creating and Managing Test Cases in Zephyr

A. Creating a Test Case in Zephyr

1. Navigate to **Jira → Test Cases → Create New Test**
2. Add **Test Steps** and **Expected Results**
3. Link the test case to a **Jira Story or Bug**
4. Assign the test case to a **QA Engineer**

Example Test Case for User Authentication

Step	Action	Expected Result
1	Navigate to /login page	Login form is visible
2	Enter valid credentials and click "Login"	User is redirected to the dashboard

3	Enter invalid credentials	"Invalid username/password" error appears

■ **Now, test cases are directly linked to Jira issues!**

---

4. Automating Test Execution with Zephyr + CI/CD

Zephyr integrates with **Jenkins, GitHub Actions, and Bitbucket Pipelines** to automate test execution.

■ **Example Workflow:**

1. Developer pushes code to **GitHub**
2. CI/CD pipeline triggers **automated tests**
3. Zephyr updates Jira issues with test **pass/fail status**
4. Failed tests reopen related Jira issues

■ **Now, QA testing is fully integrated into Jira workflows!**

Best Practices for Extending Jira with Marketplace Apps

■ **1. Choose Apps That Solve a Specific Problem**

- Avoid unnecessary complexity—select apps based on team needs.
- Example: **Use Zephyr only if test management is required inside Jira.**

■ **2. Automate Repetitive Tasks with ScriptRunner**

- Use scripts to auto-assign issues, track overdue tasks, and streamline workflows.

■ **3. Keep Jira Lightweight**

- Avoid installing **too many plugins** to prevent performance issues.

■ **4. Regularly Review App Usage**

- Assess whether installed apps are providing value and remove unused ones.

Conclusion

By extending Jira with **ScriptRunner and Zephyr**, development teams can:

✔ **Automate workflows and bulk update Jira issues with ScriptRunner**
✔ **Enhance test management by executing and tracking tests inside Jira with Zephyr**
✔ **Extend JQL capabilities for advanced reporting and searches**
✔ **Integrate CI/CD pipelines to track automated testing inside Jira**

By leveraging **Jira Marketplace Apps**, teams can **customize Jira to fit their exact needs**, improving efficiency, automation, and collaboration.

Building Custom Integrations with Jira REST API

Jira's **REST API** allows developers to extend its capabilities by **integrating with external tools, automating workflows, and retrieving Jira data programmatically**. Whether you need to **sync Jira with internal systems, automate issue management, or create custom dashboards**, the Jira REST API provides the flexibility to **customize and optimize your development processes**.

By leveraging the Jira REST API, teams can:

■ **Create, update, and manage Jira issues programmatically**
■ **Automate repetitive workflows such as transitions and notifications**
■ **Integrate Jira with third-party tools (CI/CD, reporting, messaging apps, etc.)**
■ **Extract and analyze Jira data for reporting and business intelligence**

In this chapter, you'll learn:

- **How to authenticate and interact with the Jira REST API**
- **How to create, update, and retrieve Jira issues using API requests**
- **How to automate workflows and integrate with external systems**
- **Best practices for securing and optimizing Jira API usage**

By the end of this chapter, you'll have the knowledge to **build powerful integrations that enhance Jira's functionality** and streamline your development processes.

Understanding Jira REST API Basics

1. How the Jira REST API Works

Jira's REST API is a **RESTful web service** that follows standard HTTP methods such as:

HTTP Method	Purpose	Example API Call
GET	Retrieve data	Get issue details
POST	Create new data	Create a new issue
PUT	Update existing data	Update issue fields
DELETE	Remove data	Delete an issue

■ **Base URL Format:**

https://yourcompany.atlassian.net/rest/api/3/

(`/api/3/` is used for Jira Cloud, while `/api/2/` is used for older versions.)

---

2. Authenticating API Requests

Before making API requests, you need to authenticate using **Basic Authentication** or **OAuth 2.0**.

A. Basic Authentication (Using API Token)

1. **Generate an API Token:**
   - Go to **Jira → Account Settings → Security → Create API Token**
   - Copy the generated token
2. **Send API Requests with Authentication**
   - Use the API token as the password, with your Jira email as the username

Example: Making an API Call with cURL

```
curl --request GET \
  --url "https://yourcompany.atlassian.net/rest/api/3/issue/JIRA-123" \
  --user "your-email@example.com:your-api-token" \
  --header "Accept: application/json"
```

■ Now, you can fetch Jira issue details securely!

Creating and Updating Jira Issues with the API

1. Creating a New Jira Issue via API

To create an issue programmatically, send a **POST request** with issue details in JSON format.

Example API Request (Create Issue in Jira)

```
curl --request POST \
  --url "https://yourcompany.atlassian.net/rest/api/3/issue/" \
  --user "your-email@example.com:your-api-token" \
  --header "Accept: application/json" \
  --header "Content-Type: application/json" \
  --data '{
    "fields": {
      "project": { "key": "DEV" },
      "summary": "Bug in authentication system",
      "description": "Users cannot log in with valid credentials.",
      "issuetype": { "name": "Bug" }
    }
}'
```

■ Jira will return the new issue key (e.g., "DEV-101").

---

2. Updating an Existing Jira Issue

To update an issue, use a **PUT request** with the issue ID and the updated fields.

Example API Request (Update Issue Summary)

```
curl --request PUT \
  --url "https://yourcompany.atlassian.net/rest/api/3/issue/JIRA-123" \
  --user "your-email@example.com:your-api-token" \
  --header "Accept: application/json" \
  --header "Content-Type: application/json" \
  --data '{
    "fields": {
```

```
        "summary": "Updated bug report for login issue"
    }
 }'
```

■ Now, the Jira issue summary is updated programmatically!

Automating Workflows with Jira API

1. Auto-Transition Issues Based on External Events

You can automate **issue status changes** based on external triggers, such as:

- **Moving an issue to "In Progress" when a developer starts coding**
- **Transitioning a bug to "Resolved" when a fix is deployed in CI/CD**

Example API Request (Transition Issue to "In Progress")

```
curl --request POST \
  --url
"https://yourcompany.atlassian.net/rest/api/3/issue/JIRA-123/transitions" \
  --user "your-email@example.com:your-api-token" \
  --header "Accept: application/json" \
  --header "Content-Type: application/json" \
  --data '{
    "transition": { "id": "21" }
 }'
```

(*Use the "GET transitions" API to find valid transition IDs for your workflow.*)

■ Now, Jira issues move automatically based on external triggers!

---

2. Integrating Jira with Slack for Issue Notifications

To send **Slack notifications when a new issue is created**, use the Jira API with a Slack webhook.

Example API Request (Send Slack Notification for New Issues)

```
curl -X POST -H 'Content-type: application/json' --data '{
  "text": "🚀 New Jira Issue Created: *JIRA-123*\nSummary: Authentication
Bug\nView: <https://yourcompany.atlassian.net/browse/JIRA-123>"
}' https://hooks.slack.com/services/YOUR/SLACK/WEBHOOK
```

■ Now, your team gets instant Slack notifications for new Jira issues!

Extracting Jira Data for Reporting

Jira API allows teams to fetch **real-time issue data** and generate custom reports.

1. Retrieving Issues for a Sprint or Epic

Example API Request (Get Issues from Sprint 10)

```
curl --request GET \
  --url "https://yourcompany.atlassian.net/rest/api/3/search?jql=sprint=10" \
  --user "your-email@example.com:your-api-token" \
  --header "Accept: application/json"
```

■ Now, all Sprint 10 issues can be used for analysis!

Best Practices for Secure and Efficient Jira API Usage

■ 1. Use API Tokens Instead of Passwords

- Avoid **hardcoding credentials**—use API tokens for security.

■ 2. Limit API Requests to Prevent Rate Limiting

- Jira **limits API requests per user**—batch requests when possible.

■ 3. Automate and Schedule API Calls

- Use **cron jobs** or **CI/CD pipelines** to run API tasks at set intervals.

■ 4. Store API Responses for Faster Processing

- Cache Jira API responses to **reduce redundant calls** and improve performance.

■ 5. Secure API Calls with OAuth 2.0 for Enterprise Usage

- Use **OAuth authentication** for large-scale, multi-user integrations.

Conclusion

By leveraging **Jira's REST API**, development teams can:

✔ **Automate issue creation, updates, and transitions**
✔ **Integrate Jira with CI/CD, Slack, and external tools**
✔ **Extract and analyze Jira data for reporting and insights**
✔ **Enhance security and efficiency with best practices**

With custom **Jira API integrations**, teams can build **tailored solutions** that streamline workflows, enhance visibility, and improve productivity.

Part 6:
Best Practices for Developers

Writing Effective User Stories and Acceptance Criteria

In Agile development, **user stories** provide a structured way to define requirements from the user's perspective. A well-written user story ensures **clear communication** between developers, testers, and product managers, reducing misunderstandings and unnecessary rework.

Equally important are **acceptance criteria**, which define the conditions that a user story must meet to be considered complete. **Clear, testable acceptance criteria** help developers deliver exactly what is expected and allow QA teams to verify functionality efficiently.

By mastering **user stories and acceptance criteria**, teams can:

■ **Improve requirement clarity** and reduce misinterpretations
■ **Ensure feature completeness** before moving a story to "Done"
■ **Facilitate better test case writing** for QA teams
■ **Streamline sprint planning** with well-defined, estimable tasks

In this chapter, you'll learn:

- **The structure of a good user story**
- **How to write effective acceptance criteria**
- **Using Jira to manage user stories efficiently**
- **Best practices for writing high-quality user stories**

By the end, you'll be able to **craft actionable user stories that improve development efficiency** and **enhance collaboration** across teams.

Understanding User Stories

1. What Is a User Story?

A **user story** is a **short, simple description** of a feature or requirement, told from the perspective of the user.

■ **Format of a User Story (The "INVEST" Model)**

A good user story follows the **INVEST** principle:

Principle	Description	Example
I - Independent	Should be self-contained and not dependent on another story	"As a user, I can reset my password without needing to contact support."

N - Negotiable	Can be refined and adjusted during discussions	"The password reset link should expire after 24 hours."
V - Valuable	Delivers clear value to the end-user	"As a user, I want to be able to filter search results so I can find relevant items faster."
E - Estimable	Can be sized appropriately for development	A story that is too vague (e.g., "Improve website UX") is hard to estimate.
S - Small	Should fit within a sprint	"Implement dark mode toggle for the settings page."
T - Testable	Should have clear success criteria	"The user should receive an email confirmation upon successful registration."

■ Basic User Story Template:

As a [user role],
I want to [perform an action],
So that [I achieve a goal].

■ Example of a Good User Story:

As a customer,
I want to receive an email notification when my order ships,
So that I can track my delivery status.

⊘ Example of a Poor User Story:

As a user, I want email notifications.

(*Too vague—lacks details on purpose and functionality.*)

Writing Effective Acceptance Criteria

1. What Are Acceptance Criteria?

Acceptance criteria define the **conditions that a feature must meet** before it is considered complete. They ensure:

✔ **Alignment between developers, testers, and stakeholders**
✔ **Features are testable and meet business goals**
✔ **Clear definitions of "Done" to prevent scope creep**

2. Types of Acceptance Criteria

■ Scenario-Based (Given-When-Then Format - BDD Style)

Given [context],

When [action is performed],
Then [expected outcome occurs].

Example:

Given a user has added items to their cart,
When they proceed to checkout,
Then they should see a summary of their selected items.

■ Rule-Based Acceptance Criteria

✔ Defines specific conditions that must be met.

Example:

- The password must be at least 8 characters long.
- Users must receive a confirmation email after registration.
- The system should prevent duplicate email registrations.

■ Checklist-Based Criteria

✔ Useful for UI/UX requirements.

Example:

- [ ] The button color should match the theme.
- [ ] The page should be mobile-responsive.
- [ ] Error messages should be clear and actionable.

Using Jira for User Stories and Acceptance Criteria

1. Creating a User Story in Jira

1. Navigate to your **Jira project**.
2. Click **"Create"** and select **"Story"** as the issue type.
3. Use the **user story format** in the **Summary** field.
4. Add **Acceptance Criteria** in the **Description** field.
5. Assign to a **developer** and set a **priority**.
6. Add **Story Points** for estimation (e.g., 3 points for medium complexity).

■ Example Jira User Story Entry:

Field	Value
Summary	"As a user, I want to reset my password via email."
Description	"When a user forgets their password, they should be able to reset it by receiving an email link."
Acceptance Criteria	- Users receive a reset email within 1 minute. - The reset link expires in 24 hours.

	- Users can set a new password only once per request.
Story Points	3
Priority	High

■ Best Practice:

- Link related **Bugs and Test Cases** to the story for tracking.
- Use **Jira Labels** (e.g., `authentication`, `ui-improvement`) to categorize stories.

Best Practices for Writing High-Quality User Stories

■ 1. Keep User Stories Focused and Concise

- **One feature per story** to avoid complexity.
- Example: Separate "Sign-up flow" from "Password reset flow."

■ 2. Write Stories Collaboratively

- Developers, testers, and product owners should refine stories together.

■ 3. Define Clear Acceptance Criteria

- Ensures that **developers and QA teams** know what to expect.

■ 4. Make Stories Testable

- Every story should be **measurable** (e.g., "Page loads in under 3 seconds").

■ 5. Break Down Large Stories into Smaller Ones

- Example:
    - **Epic:** "User Authentication System"
    - **Story 1:** "As a user, I can sign up using my email."
    - **Story 2:** "As a user, I can log in with my credentials."
    - **Story 3:** "As a user, I can reset my password via email."

■ **Now, stories are easier to manage and deliver within a sprint!**

Conclusion

By following structured **user story writing and acceptance criteria**, teams can:

✔ **Ensure better communication between stakeholders**
✔ **Improve development efficiency with well-defined requirements**
✔ **Reduce misunderstandings and unnecessary work**
✔ **Enhance testability and overall software quality**

With **Jira's issue tracking**, teams can **effectively manage user stories**, ensuring smooth development cycles and well-organized sprints.

Agile Estimation Techniques in Jira

Estimating work in Agile software development helps teams **plan sprints, allocate resources, and predict delivery timelines**. Jira provides **various estimation techniques** that help teams break down work into measurable units, ensuring a smooth and predictable workflow.

By using Agile estimation techniques in Jira, teams can:

■ **Improve sprint planning accuracy**
■ **Avoid overloading developers with unrealistic workloads**
■ **Track team velocity for better forecasting**
■ **Ensure alignment between developers, product owners, and stakeholders**

In this chapter, you'll learn:

- **Why estimation is important in Agile workflows**
- **Different Agile estimation techniques used in Jira**
- **How to implement story points, t-shirt sizing, and time estimates in Jira**
- **Best practices for improving estimation accuracy**

By the end, you'll be able to **apply the right estimation techniques** to make your Jira-based development workflows more predictable and efficient.

Understanding Agile Estimation

1. Why Do We Estimate in Agile?

Estimation in Agile is **not about exact precision**—it's about making **reasonable approximations** to help with:

✔ **Sprint Planning** – Helps teams commit to realistic workloads.
✔ **Release Forecasting** – Predicts when features will be completed.
✔ **Team Performance Measurement** – Tracks **velocity** (amount of work completed per sprint).

■ **Best Practice:** Focus on **relative estimation** rather than trying to predict exact hours of effort.

2. Common Agile Estimation Techniques

Technique	Best For	Example in Jira
Story Points	Estimating effort relative to other tasks	"This task is 5 story points, similar to a previous 5-point task."
T-Shirt Sizing	Quick high-level estimation before breaking down tasks	"This feature is a 'Medium' effort item."
Time-Based Estimation	Estimating actual hours or days required	"This bug fix will take approximately 6 hours."
Affinity Estimation	Categorizing tasks into groups based on effort	"Sorting backlog tasks into similar effort levels."

Implementing Story Points in Jira

1. What Are Story Points?

Story points measure **effort**, **complexity**, and **risk**, rather than time.

💡 **Example Scale:**

Story Points	Effort Description	Example Task
1	Very simple task	Change a button color
3	Small task	Add a new form field
5	Medium task	Implement a login system
8	Large task	Develop a new checkout process
13+	Very complex	Migrate database infrastructure

■ **Best Practice:**

- **Do NOT equate story points to hours.**
- Keep story points **relative** (e.g., "This feature is twice as complex as that one").

2. Enabling Story Points in Jira

1. Go to **Jira → Project Settings → Issues**
2. Select **Custom Fields** → Add a new **Story Points** field
3. Assign **Story Points** as an **Estimation** field in your Jira board

■ **Now, your team can estimate tasks using story points!**

3. Using Story Points for Sprint Planning

1. **Break down tasks into manageable sizes**
2. Assign **story points** based on **relative complexity**
3. Use Jira's **Sprint Planning Board** to check if the workload is **realistic**

■ **Example:** If the team completes **30 story points per sprint**, then the upcoming sprint should contain around **30 points of work**.

Using T-Shirt Sizing for Quick Estimation

1. What Is T-Shirt Sizing?

T-shirt sizing is a **fast, high-level estimation method** that categorizes tasks as:

✔ **XS (Extra Small)** – Trivial tasks
✔ **S (Small)** – Minor changes
✔ **M (Medium)** – Regular-sized feature
✔ **L (Large)** – Significant work
✔ **XL (Extra Large)** – Needs breaking down

◼ **Best Practice:**

- Use T-shirt sizing during **backlog refinement** before assigning story points.
- Convert **M/L/XL tasks into smaller, more manageable stories** before sprint planning.

2. How to Use T-Shirt Sizing in Jira

1. Create a **Custom Field** named **T-Shirt Size**.
2. Use **Labels or Dropdowns** to categorize tasks as **XS, S, M, L, or XL**.
3. Use Jira's **Quick Filters** to sort issues by **T-Shirt Size**.

◼ **Now, your team can quickly size work without overcomplicating estimates.**

Using Time-Based Estimation in Jira

1. What Is Time-Based Estimation?

Time-based estimation assigns **actual hours or days** to tasks. It's useful for:

✔ **Bug fixes and technical tasks**
✔ **Non-development tasks (e.g., documentation, design work)**
✔ **Teams that prefer traditional tracking**

◼ **Best Practice:** Use time estimates **only when necessary** (e.g., critical deadlines).

2. Enabling Time Estimates in Jira

1. Go to **Jira Board → Configure Fields**
2. Enable **Time Tracking**
3. Add estimates under **Original Estimate** field

◼ **Now, Jira can track actual vs. estimated time per issue.**

Using Affinity Estimation for Large Backlogs

1. What Is Affinity Estimation?

Affinity estimation helps teams **quickly sort backlog items** into categories based on effort.

◼ **Steps:**

1. Gather the team and **review all backlog items**.
2. Group similar tasks together into **buckets (small, medium, large, etc.)**.

3. Adjust based on team discussions.

💡 **Example Jira Workflow:**

- Use **Swimlanes in Jira Boards** to organize tasks into **effort categories**.

Best Practices for Agile Estimation

■ **1. Use Story Points for Feature Development**

- Avoid **time-based estimates** for large projects.

■ **2. Keep Estimates Relative, Not Absolute**

- Example: "Feature A is twice as complex as Feature B."

■ **3. Review and Adjust Estimates Regularly**

- Check **past estimations** to improve accuracy.

■ **4. Use T-Shirt Sizing for Quick Estimation**

- Before diving into detailed story points, **size work first**.

■ **5. Keep Stories Small and Estimable**

- **Break down large stories** before assigning story points.

Conclusion

By applying **Agile estimation techniques in Jira**, teams can:

✔ **Improve sprint planning accuracy with story points**
✔ **Use T-shirt sizing for fast, high-level estimates**
✔ **Track time estimates for tasks that require deadlines**
✔ **Group similar tasks with affinity estimation**

With the right estimation approach, Jira becomes a **powerful planning tool**, ensuring **realistic workloads and predictable delivery**.

Balancing Technical Debt vs. Feature Development

Every software development team faces the challenge of **balancing technical debt and feature development**. While **new features** drive product growth and user satisfaction, **technical debt** accumulates as shortcuts, outdated code, and unresolved bugs slow down future development.

If left unchecked, technical debt can:

✘ **Increase maintenance costs**
✘ **Reduce development velocity**
✘ **Cause regressions and poor user experience**
✘ **Demotivate developers by forcing them to work with bad code**

However, focusing only on **paying down technical debt** without shipping features can stall innovation. The key is to find **the right balance**—ensuring product growth while keeping the codebase maintainable.

In this chapter, you'll learn:

- **What technical debt is and why it happens**
- **How to track and manage technical debt in Jira**
- **Strategies to balance tech debt with feature delivery**
- **Best practices for maintaining a scalable, maintainable codebase**

By the end, you'll be equipped with the tools to **prioritize and manage technical debt effectively in Jira**, ensuring your team builds sustainable software without compromising innovation.

Understanding Technical Debt

1. What Is Technical Debt?

Technical debt is the **cost of taking shortcuts** in development, which leads to future rework. It's like accumulating **financial debt**—if you don't pay it off regularly, the **"interest" (extra effort needed to fix issues later) grows**.

■ **Common Causes of Technical Debt:**

Cause	Example
Rushed Development	Skipping best practices to meet a deadline
Outdated Code	Legacy code that isn't compatible with new frameworks
Lack of Documentation	Developers struggle to understand past decisions
Poorly Written Tests	Low test coverage increases risk of regressions
Hardcoded Logic	Code that lacks flexibility and scalability

■ **Types of Technical Debt:**

1. **Planned Debt** – Intentional shortcuts for faster delivery (e.g., MVP development).
2. **Unintentional Debt** – Caused by bad design or lack of experience.
3. **Bit Rot Debt** – Accumulates as code deteriorates over time due to lack of maintenance.

Tracking Technical Debt in Jira

Jira helps teams **track and manage technical debt** by:

✔ **Creating dedicated issues for tech debt**
✔ **Tagging and prioritizing tech debt alongside feature work**
✔ **Using Jira dashboards to monitor tech debt levels**

1. Creating a Technical Debt Issue in Jira

1. Navigate to your **Jira project**
2. Click **Create Issue**
3. Use the **Issue Type**: "Technical Debt"
4. Write a **clear description** of the debt
5. Assign **Priority** (High, Medium, Low)
6. Label it with **tags like `tech-debt`, `refactoring-needed`**
7. Link it to relevant **features or bugs**

■ **Example Jira Technical Debt Issue**

Field	Value
Summary	"Refactor authentication service to use OAuth 2.0"
Description	"The current authentication system is outdated and lacks security best practices."
Priority	High
Labels	`tech-debt, security`
Linked Issues	"Feature: SSO Login"
Story Points	8

2. Using Jira Dashboards to Monitor Technical Debt

Set up a **Jira Dashboard** to track technical debt across projects.

■ **Recommended Dashboard Widgets:**

- **Pie Chart** – Breakdown of technical debt by priority
- **Filter Results** – Show unresolved `tech-debt` issues
- **Sprint Report** – Track completed vs. remaining tech debt items
- **Velocity Chart** – Compare tech debt resolution rate vs. feature development

■ **Best Practice:** Review tech debt issues **during sprint planning** and allocate time for fixing them.

Strategies to Balance Technical Debt vs. Feature Development

1. The 80/20 Rule for Sprint Planning

A good rule of thumb is to allocate **80% of sprint capacity for new features** and **20% for technical debt resolution**.

Sprint Work Type	Percentage
New Feature Development	80%
Technical Debt / Refactoring	20%

■ **Best Practice:** Plan **dedicated tech debt sprints** every few months for larger refactors.

---

2. Define "Definition of Done" to Prevent More Debt

Ensure that every Jira issue follows a strict **Definition of Done (DoD)** to **avoid accumulating new technical debt**.

■ **Example "Definition of Done" Checklist:**

☑ Code follows team's style guide
☑ Unit tests cover at least 80% of new code
☑ No TODO or commented-out code left behind
☑ Proper documentation is added

■ **Best Practice:** Use **Jira Workflow Automation** to enforce DoD.

---

3. Identify High-Risk Technical Debt Using Jira Reports

Use Jira's **Cumulative Flow Diagram** and **Velocity Chart** to spot technical debt slowing down development.

✔ **Cumulative Flow Diagram** – Shows if issues are piling up in "In Progress"
✔ **Velocity Chart** – If velocity is declining, tech debt may be the cause

■ **Best Practice:** Schedule a **technical debt review meeting** every sprint.

---

4. Refactor Opportunistically

Instead of full-scale rewrites, **incrementally refactor** when working on related features.

■ **Example Jira Workflow for Opportunistic Refactoring:**

1. Identify **legacy code** while developing a new feature.
2. Create a **subtask in Jira** labeled `tech-debt`.
3. Allocate **time within the sprint** to refactor that small portion.
4. Test and deploy the **new feature + refactored code** together.

■ **Best Practice:** Always **document refactored areas** in Jira for future reference.

---

5. Align Technical Debt with Business Goals

Business teams often **prioritize features over code maintenance**. To justify tech debt work:

■ **Link tech debt issues to business impact:**

- "Fixing this will reduce bug reports by 30%."
- "Refactoring will improve page load speed, reducing bounce rate."

■ **Use Jira reports to quantify impact:**

- **Bug Density** – Number of defects caused by tech debt.
- **Cycle Time** – Slowdown caused by outdated code.

Best Practices for Managing Technical Debt

■ **1. Track and Prioritize Tech Debt in Jira**

- Use **labels (`tech-debt`, `refactor-needed`)** to track issues.

■ **2. Set Up a Regular Tech Debt Review**

- Conduct a **"Tech Debt Grooming" session** every sprint.

■ **3. Balance Feature Development and Tech Debt Fixes**

- Follow the **80/20 rule** (80% new features, 20% debt resolution).

■ **4. Avoid Creating More Technical Debt**

- Enforce a **Definition of Done (DoD)** for all code changes.

■ **5. Justify Technical Debt Fixes with Data**

- Use Jira **reports and metrics** to prove business impact.

Conclusion

Balancing **technical debt and feature development** is essential for long-term product sustainability.

✔ **Use Jira to track and prioritize tech debt alongside new features.**
✔ **Apply the 80/20 rule to allocate time for maintenance.**
✔ **Refactor incrementally rather than rewriting everything at once.**
✔ **Use Jira reports to measure and communicate the impact of technical debt.**

By integrating **technical debt management into your development workflow**, your team can **build scalable, maintainable software** while continuing to deliver new features.

Collaboration Tips for Remote Development Teams

With the rise of **remote work**, development teams are increasingly distributed across multiple time zones and locations. While remote development offers **flexibility and access to global talent**, it also presents challenges such as **communication gaps, reduced visibility, and coordination issues**.

Jira, when used effectively, becomes **the central hub for remote teams**, ensuring **task visibility, collaboration, and alignment** across different workstreams.

By implementing **remote-friendly collaboration strategies in Jira**, teams can:

■ **Ensure clear communication across time zones**
■ **Improve task visibility and accountability**
■ **Streamline Agile workflows with automation**
■ **Maintain engagement and avoid developer isolation**

In this chapter, you'll learn:

- **How to set up Jira for remote collaboration**
- **Best practices for communication and async work in Jira**
- **How to track progress and maintain alignment across time zones**
- **Tips for improving engagement and productivity in remote teams**

By the end, you'll be equipped to **optimize Jira for remote teamwork**, ensuring seamless collaboration and efficient development cycles.

Setting Up Jira for Remote Team Collaboration

1. Use a Consistent Jira Workflow

Remote teams rely on **asynchronous work**, meaning **everyone should know what's expected at each stage** of the development process.

■ **Best Practices for Jira Workflows in Remote Teams:**

✔ **Define clear status transitions** – Avoid confusion by making workflow steps explicit (e.g., "To Do → In Progress → Code Review → Done").
✔ **Use automation** – Set up **auto-assignments, notifications, and reminders** for updates.
✔ **Create a workflow diagram** – Ensure all team members understand Jira's issue flow.

---

2. Enable Time Zone Awareness in Jira

When working across different time zones:

✔ Set **Jira's time zone settings** to reflect **each user's local time**.
✔ Add **time zone labels** (e.g., [EST], [PST]) to sprint planning sessions.
✔ Use Jira's **"Due Date" and "Assignee" filters** to track work across global teams.

■ **Best Practice:** Set up a **Jira calendar view** to track important deadlines across time zones.

---

3. Use Jira Boards for Transparency

Jira boards (Scrum or Kanban) help remote teams track work **visually**.

■ **Best Practices for Remote Teams:**

✔ Use **Swimlanes** for better organization (e.g., per team, per priority).
✔ Use **Jira Labels** (`frontend`, `backend`, `urgent`) to categorize work.
✔ Set up **Jira Dashboards** for real-time project status updates.

■ **Example Kanban Board Setup for a Remote Team:**

Column	Description
Backlog	Tasks planned for future sprints
To Do	Tasks ready for development
In Progress	Tasks currently being worked on
Code Review	Tasks awaiting peer review
QA Testing	Tasks in the testing phase
Done	Completed tasks

■ **Best Practice:** Use **WIP (Work In Progress) limits** to prevent team overload.

Communication and Async Work in Jira

1. Use Jira Comments Instead of Email

Remote teams should use Jira **as the primary source of communication** instead of emails or chat for issue-related discussions.

■ **Best Practices for Jira Comments:**

✔ **Tag teammates (@mention) for quick updates**
✔ **Use bullet points for clarity**
✔ **Link related Jira issues for reference**
✔ **Keep updates concise and actionable**

■ **Example of a Good Jira Comment:**

@JohnDoe Can you confirm if the API fix in JIRA-456 resolves the login bug?
Once confirmed, we can move this issue to QA.

🚫 **Example of a Bad Jira Comment:**

Hey, check this out when you have time.

(Lacks clarity and actionability.)

---

2. Document Key Decisions in Jira

Since remote teams often work asynchronously, **decisions made in meetings or Slack should be documented in Jira**.

🟦 **Example Documentation in Jira Issue Description:**

Discussion Summary (Sprint Planning - Jan 15th):
- Feature A will be prioritized for Sprint 10
- Backend refactor will be handled in Sprint 11
- Deployment is scheduled for Feb 1st

---

3. Automate Notifications for Task Updates

Jira's **Slack and Microsoft Teams integrations** can keep remote teams updated **without constant check-ins**.

🟦 **Set Up Jira Notifications for Remote Teams:**

- **Send Slack alerts when an issue is moved to "In Progress".**
- **Auto-tag assignees in comments when their task is blocked.**
- **Notify stakeholders when a task is marked "Done".**

🟦 **Best Practice:** Use Jira's **webhooks** to integrate with Slack, MS Teams, and email.

Tracking Progress and Maintaining Alignment

1. Set Up Jira Dashboards for Visibility

Jira Dashboards provide **real-time insights** into progress, helping remote teams stay aligned.

🟦 **Essential Widgets for Remote Teams:**
✔ **Sprint Burndown Chart** – Tracks remaining work per sprint
✔ **Team Velocity Chart** – Measures how much work gets done per sprint
✔ **Issue Heatmap** – Shows high-priority tasks that need attention

🟦 **Best Practice:** Review Jira dashboards **in weekly standups** to keep everyone aligned.

---

2. Use Jira Reports for Async Standups

Instead of daily standup meetings, remote teams can **use Jira comments for async standups**.

🟦 **Example Jira Async Standup Format:**

Yesterday: Worked on API authentication issue.
Today: Fixing database migration bug.
Blocked By: Waiting on frontend team to confirm UI changes.

🟦 **Best Practice:** Create a **Jira filter** for "Blocked Issues" to track dependencies.

Improving Engagement and Productivity in Remote Teams

1. Recognize Contributions with Jira Reports

Remote teams often lack the **visibility of in-office praise**. Use Jira to **highlight achievements**:

■ **Ways to Recognize Contributions in Jira:**
✔ **Feature Completion Report** – Celebrate major milestones.
✔ **Team Performance Chart** – Highlight top contributors.
✔ **"Kudos" Comments** – Acknowledge good work in Jira comments.

■ **Best Practice:** Encourage **team leads** to leave positive feedback on Jira tickets.

2. Prevent Burnout by Tracking Workload in Jira

Remote developers often struggle with **work-life balance**.

■ **Best Practices for Preventing Burnout:**
✔ **Limit work-in-progress (WIP) tasks** to **2-3 per developer**.
✔ Use Jira's **Workload Reports** to ensure **no one is overloaded**.
✔ **Encourage time-off tracking** by logging vacation days in Jira.

■ **Best Practice:** Use Jira's **Capacity Planning** tool to allocate workload fairly.

3. Conduct Regular Retrospectives in Jira

Every sprint should include a **retrospective to improve collaboration**.

■ **Example Jira Retrospective Board:**

Column	Examples
What Went Well?	"Jira integration with Slack improved updates."
What Can Be Improved?	"Too many issues were unassigned."
Action Items	"Ensure every Jira issue has an owner by sprint start."

■ **Best Practice:** Document retrospective notes in a **Jira Confluence page** for future reference.

Conclusion

By leveraging **Jira's features and remote-friendly workflows**, development teams can:

✔ **Ensure clear communication across time zones**
✔ **Maintain visibility on tasks and progress**
✔ **Use automation to reduce manual follow-ups**
✔ **Recognize and support team members in a remote setting**

With the right **Jira configurations and best practices**, remote development teams can collaborate effectively while maintaining productivity and engagement.

Part 7:
Troubleshooting and Optimization

Debugging Common Jira Configuration Errors

Jira is a **powerful and flexible** issue-tracking system, but its **complex configurations** can sometimes lead to errors that disrupt development workflows. Incorrect permissions, misconfigured workflows, or API issues can prevent teams from **tracking work efficiently**.

By understanding **common Jira configuration errors and their solutions**, teams can:

■ **Resolve issues quickly** to minimize downtime
■ **Maintain smooth workflows** for developers
■ **Prevent recurring errors** with best practices
■ **Enhance Jira's performance and usability**

In this chapter, we'll explore:

- **Common Jira configuration errors and their causes**
- **Step-by-step solutions to fix them**
- **Best practices to prevent these errors**

By the end, you'll be equipped to **troubleshoot and optimize Jira effectively**, ensuring your development team experiences minimal disruptions.

---

1. Common Jira Configuration Errors and Fixes

1.1. Issue Creation Errors (Cannot Create an Issue)

🔔 **Error Message:**
"You do not have permission to create issues in this project."

🔍 **Possible Causes:**
✔ Insufficient permissions for the user.
✔ Issue type is not linked to the project workflow.
✔ Required fields in the issue creation screen are misconfigured.

🛠 **Solution:**

1. **Check User Permissions:**
   ○ Navigate to **Jira Settings → Issues → Permission Schemes**.
   ○ Ensure the user has the "Create Issues" permission.
2. **Verify Issue Type Scheme:**
   ○ Go to **Project Settings → Issue Types** and ensure the issue type is included.
3. **Check Mandatory Fields:**
   ○ Go to **Jira Settings → Issues → Field Configurations** and verify that required fields are correctly set.

■ **Best Practice:** Use **Permission Helper (Jira Admin Tools → Permission Helper)** to debug permission issues.

1.2. Workflow Errors (Cannot Transition Issues)

🔔 **Error Message:**
"You do not have permission to transition this issue."

🔍 **Possible Causes:**
✔ Workflow transition requires a specific user role.
✔ The transition has a validation condition that isn't met.
✔ A post-function is blocking the transition.

🔧 **Solution:**

1. **Check Workflow Conditions:**
   ○ Go to **Jira Settings → Issues → Workflows**.
   ○ Select the project workflow and review the conditions.
2. **Modify Transition Permissions:**
   ○ Ensure the "Transition Issues" permission is assigned to the correct roles in **Project Settings → Permissions**.
3. **Verify Post-Functions and Validators:**
   ○ Navigate to **Workflows → Edit Workflow**.
   ○ Remove unnecessary validators or post-functions that may be causing issues.

■ **Best Practice:** Avoid **overcomplicating workflows**—keep conditions minimal for smoother transitions.

1.3. Notification Issues (Users Not Receiving Emails)

🔔 **Error:**
"Users do not receive Jira notifications."

🔍 **Possible Causes:**
✔ Notification scheme is not set up correctly.
✔ Users have disabled email notifications.
✔ Emails are getting blocked by spam filters.

🔧 **Solution:**

1. **Check Notification Scheme:**
   ○ Go to **Jira Settings → Issues → Notification Schemes**.
   ○ Ensure that the correct events (Issue Created, Issue Updated, etc.) have recipients assigned.
2. **Verify User Notification Preferences:**
   ○ Instruct users to check **Profile Settings → Email Notifications**.
3. **Test Email Delivery:**
   ○ Go to **Jira System Settings → Outgoing Mail**.
   ○ Click **Test Connection** to check if Jira can send emails.

■ **Best Practice:** Use a **Jira notification log plugin** to track email delivery issues.

1.4. Jira Automation Errors (Automation Rules Not Working)

🔔 **Error Message:**
"Rule execution failed: Insufficient permissions or missing field."

🔍 **Possible Causes:**
✔ The automation rule lacks permission to perform an action.
✔ The rule is referencing a missing field.
✔ The automation actor (user executing the rule) does not have sufficient permissions.

⚒ **Solution:**

1. **Verify Rule Permissions:**
   - Go to **Jira Settings → Automation**.
   - Ensure the automation **actor** has the necessary permissions.
2. **Check the Rule Execution Log:**
   - Navigate to **Automation → Audit Log**.
   - Look for errors and missing fields in execution logs.
3. **Test Rule with a Sample Issue:**
   - Use the **"Run Rule Manually"** feature to debug errors.

◼ **Best Practice:** Always **test automation rules** on a staging environment before deploying in production.

1.5. Jira Performance Issues (Slow Load Times, Freezing UI)

🔔 **Error:**
"Jira is running slowly, and pages take too long to load."

🔍 **Possible Causes:**
✔ Too many active plugins slowing down performance.
✔ Large backlog or too many open issues in a project.
✔ Inefficient JQL queries slowing down reports.

⚒ **Solution:**

1. **Disable Unnecessary Plugins:**
   - Go to **Jira Administration → Manage Apps**.
   - Disable unused marketplace apps.
2. **Archive Old Issues:**
   - Use **Jira's Archive feature** to remove completed issues from active queries.
3. **Optimize JQL Queries:**
   - Avoid `"ORDER BY"` in large datasets.
   - Use **indexed fields** (e.g., `project = DEV AND status = "In Progress"` instead of `text ~ "in progress"`).

◼ **Best Practice:** Use **Jira's Application Performance Monitoring** to track slow-performing queries and plugins.

---

2. Best Practices to Prevent Jira Configuration Errors

◼ **1. Maintain a Jira Configuration Change Log**

- Keep track of **all changes** made to Jira settings to **trace back errors**.

2. Use Jira Staging Environment for Testing

- Before making changes to workflows, permissions, or automation rules, **test them in a sandbox environment**.

3. Perform Regular Permission Audits

- Ensure **new team members have the correct permissions** and **inactive users are removed**.

4. Keep Jira Workflows Simple

- Overly **complex workflows increase configuration errors**. Stick to **standard issue transitions** whenever possible.

5. Train Teams on Jira Best Practices

- Provide **documentation and training** for developers, testers, and managers to **prevent misconfigurations**.

6. Monitor Jira Logs for Errors

- Regularly check **Jira System Logs (Administration → System → Logging and Profiling)** for warnings and errors.

7. Use Jira Marketplace Apps for Debugging

- Install **Jira Admin Tools, ScriptRunner, or Performance Tuner** to **identify and resolve issues faster**.

Conclusion

By following structured **troubleshooting methods and best practices**, teams can:

✔ **Quickly resolve common Jira configuration errors**
✔ **Prevent workflow disruptions and improve efficiency**
✔ **Optimize Jira's performance for large-scale projects**
✔ **Ensure a smooth developer experience with automated debugging tools**

With **Jira properly configured and maintained**, development teams can focus on **building high-quality software without workflow bottlenecks**.

Optimizing Performance for Large-Scale Projects

Jira is a powerful tool, but as teams scale and projects grow, performance issues can arise. Large-scale projects often suffer from **slow load times, inefficient queries, and workflow bottlenecks**. Without proper optimization, Jira can become **unresponsive, difficult to navigate, and frustrating for teams**.

By **optimizing Jira for large-scale projects**, development teams can:

■ Improve **page load times and query execution speeds**
■ Ensure **efficient backlog and sprint management**
■ Prevent **database overload and workflow bottlenecks**
■ Keep Jira responsive, even with **thousands of issues and users**

In this chapter, you'll learn:

- **Common Jira performance issues and their causes**
- **Strategies to optimize Jira for large-scale projects**
- **Best practices for managing large backlogs and queries**
- **How to track and monitor Jira's performance**

By the end, you'll be able to **keep Jira fast and efficient**, even for enterprise-scale development projects.

---

1. Common Performance Issues in Large Jira Projects

1.1. Slow Page Load Times

🔋 **Symptoms:**
✔ Jira dashboards, boards, and issue pages take **longer than 5 seconds to load**.
✔ Performance worsens as **more issues, users, and teams** are added.

🔍 **Causes:**
✔ Large backlog with **too many open issues**.
✔ Excessive use of **gadget-heavy dashboards**.
✔ Inefficient JQL queries slowing down pages.

1.2. Long Query Execution Times

🔋 **Symptoms:**
✔ Filters and reports take **too long to execute**.
✔ JQL queries slow down significantly with **thousands of issues**.

🔍 **Causes:**
✔ Use of **unindexed fields** (e.g., text ~ "search term").
✔ Complex queries with multiple ORDER BY and JOIN conditions.
✔ Too many **custom fields** impacting indexing.

1.3. Workflow Bottlenecks

Symptoms:
✔ Developers struggle to transition issues efficiently.
. ✔ Workflows contain **too many conditions, validators, or post-functions**.
✔ Automation rules cause delays in issue transitions.

Causes:
✔ Overly complex workflows with **multiple conditional steps**.
✔ High number of **custom scripts and post-functions**.
✔ Misconfigured automation rules **executing redundantly**.

---

2. Strategies to Optimize Jira for Large-Scale Projects

2.1. Reduce Backlog Size and Archive Old Issues

Best Practice: Archive or delete old and unnecessary issues to keep Jira responsive.

Steps to Reduce Backlog Size:

1. **Identify Stale Issues:**
   ○ Use JQL:

   project = "XYZ" AND status = "To Do" AND updated < -180d

   ○ This finds issues that **haven't been updated in the last 180 days**.
2. **Bulk Close or Archive Issues:**
   ○ Use **Jira's bulk edit** feature to close or move issues to an archived project.

Result: Faster search queries and a more manageable backlog.

2.2. Optimize JQL Queries for Speed

Best Practice: Use **indexed fields** instead of free-text searches for faster queries.

Slow JQL Query Example:

project = "DevOps" AND text ~ "server error" ORDER BY created DESC

(*This performs a slow text search and sorts all issues.*)

Optimized JQL Query:

project = "DevOps" AND status = "Open" AND summary ~ "server error"

(*This filters by indexed fields first, making execution much faster.*)

Result: Reports and boards load **faster with optimized filters**.

2.3. Optimize Jira Workflows for Efficiency

Best Practice: Avoid **unnecessary workflow complexity** to improve performance.

■ **Steps to Optimize Workflows:**

1. **Remove redundant workflow conditions** (e.g., multiple role-based validators).
2. **Simplify transitions** by reducing **unneeded post-functions**.
3. **Use automation carefully** – excessive automation rules can slow down transitions.
4. **Monitor transition time** to identify bottlenecks.

🚀 **Result: Smoother issue transitions** and faster board performance.

2.4. Optimize Jira Dashboards and Gadgets

💡 **Best Practice:** Keep dashboards **lean** and avoid overloading with gadgets.

■ **Steps to Optimize Dashboards:**
✔ **Limit the number of gadgets** – Keep **max 5 gadgets per dashboard**.
✔ **Use simple widgets** (e.g., **Pie Charts instead of complex JQL tables**).
✔ **Enable caching for frequently used reports.**

🚀 **Result:** Faster dashboard loading times for **all team members**.

2.5. Monitor and Improve Jira Performance

💡 **Best Practice:** Track **key performance metrics** and optimize continuously.

■ **Tools for Monitoring Jira Performance:**

Tool	Use Case
Jira Application Performance Monitoring	Identifies slow-performing areas in Jira
Jira Database Health Check	Detects slow queries and indexing issues
Atlassian Jira Performance Testing Toolkit	Simulates large loads and stress tests Jira

■ **Key Metrics to Monitor:**
✔ **Average Page Load Time** – Should be **under 3 seconds**.
✔ **JQL Execution Time** – Should complete **within 2-5 seconds**.
✔ **Workflow Transition Time** – Should be **under 2 seconds per step**.

🚀 **Result:** Teams can proactively **fix performance bottlenecks before they impact users**.

---

3. Best Practices for Managing Large-Scale Jira Projects

■ **1. Archive Old Data Regularly**

- Move **completed epics and old issues** to an **archive project**.

■ **2. Use Jira Data Center for Scalability**

- If running Jira Server, consider **migrating to Jira Data Center** for **better performance at scale**.

■ **3. Avoid Excessive Custom Fields**

- Too many **custom fields slow down searches**. Keep only **essential fields**.

4. Optimize Permissions and Roles

- **Limit global permissions** and avoid too many **custom permission schemes**.

5. Schedule Regular Performance Audits

- Run **quarterly Jira performance tests** to **identify and resolve slow queries**.

6. Automate Backlog Grooming

- Use Jira automation to **close inactive issues automatically** after a set period.

7. Use Jira Cloud for Auto-Scaling

- If using Jira Server, **consider migrating to Jira Cloud** for **better auto-scaling and reduced maintenance overhead**.

Conclusion

By implementing **Jira optimization strategies**, teams can:

✔ **Keep Jira fast and responsive, even with thousands of issues**
✔ **Ensure smooth workflows and quick issue transitions**
✔ **Reduce backlog size for better search and reporting performance**
✔ **Improve dashboard and report efficiency**

With the right **performance monitoring and management strategies**, large-scale teams can **scale Jira effectively** while maintaining an efficient and high-performing development environment.

Securing Jira for Development Environments

As a **mission-critical tool for software development**, Jira stores **sensitive project data, code references, deployment details, and developer communications**. Without **proper security measures**, Jira can become **a target for cyberattacks, unauthorized access, and data leaks**.

Securing Jira is **essential** for:

■ **Protecting sensitive project and company data**
■ **Ensuring compliance with security and privacy regulations**
■ **Preventing unauthorized access to confidential information**
■ **Reducing the risk of insider threats and accidental data exposure**

In this chapter, we'll cover:

- **Common Jira security risks and how to mitigate them**
- **Best practices for user access control and permission management**
- **Securing Jira integrations and API access**
- **Backup and disaster recovery strategies for Jira data**

By the end, you'll have a **comprehensive security strategy** for keeping Jira **safe, compliant, and resilient** in a development environment.

---

1. Common Jira Security Risks and Threats

1.1. Unauthorized Access to Sensitive Data

🔍 **Risk:**
✔ Unrestricted user access exposes **confidential development information**.
✔ Lack of proper **role-based access control (RBAC)** leads to **unintended data leaks**.

🔧 **Solution:**
✔ Use **Jira permission schemes** to restrict access based on roles.
✔ **Limit admin privileges** to only essential team members.

■ Best Practice: Use the Principle of Least Privilege (PoLP) – grant only the minimum permissions needed for each role.

1.2. Weak Authentication and Password Security

🔍 **Risk:**
✔ Developers using **weak passwords** increase the risk of **credential leaks**.
✔ Lack of **Multi-Factor Authentication (MFA)** makes Jira accounts vulnerable to brute-force attacks.

🔧 **Solution:**
✔ **Enable MFA** for all Jira users.
✔ Enforce **strong password policies** using Jira's security settings.
✔ Integrate Jira with **Single Sign-On (SSO)** using **SAML, OAuth, or LDAP**.

■ Best Practice: Use **password managers** and enforce periodic **password rotation** for admin accounts.

1.3. Unsecured Jira API and Webhooks

🔍 **Risk:**
✔ API keys **hardcoded in scripts** can be **stolen and misused**.
✔ **Open or unprotected API endpoints** can be exploited by attackers.

🔧 **Solution:**
✔ Use **OAuth 2.0 authentication** instead of **basic authentication** for API access.
✔ Restrict API keys to **specific IP addresses** or **trusted applications**.
✔ Monitor **Jira webhooks** for unauthorized access attempts.

◼ **Best Practice:** Rotate API keys **regularly** and limit their **scope and expiration time**.

1.4. Exposure of Internal Data in Public Jira Projects

🔍 **Risk:**
✔ Developers may **accidentally** set a project as **public**, exposing internal data to external users.
✔ **Incorrect issue visibility settings** lead to **confidential information leaks**.

🔧 **Solution:**
✔ Go to **Jira Settings → Global Permissions** and restrict **"Browse Projects"** access.
✔ Use **Issue Security Schemes** to control who can view specific issues.
✔ Regularly audit **public vs. private project settings**.

◼ **Best Practice:** Conduct **monthly security audits** to review **access permissions** across all projects.

1.5. Lack of Jira Backup and Disaster Recovery Plan

🔍 **Risk:**
✔ No **regular backups** means data **can be lost due to accidental deletions, server failures, or cyberattacks**.
✔ Lack of **disaster recovery procedures** can cause extended downtime.

🔧 **Solution:**
✔ Enable **daily automated backups** of Jira databases and attachments.
✔ Store backups in **multiple secure locations (cloud + local storage)**.
✔ Implement a **disaster recovery plan** with a **defined Recovery Time Objective (RTO) and Recovery Point Objective (RPO)**.

◼ **Best Practice:** Test **backup restoration** quarterly to ensure **quick recovery in case of failure**.

2. Best Practices for Securing Jira

2.1. Implement Strong User Access Controls

◼ **Steps to Secure Jira User Access:**

1. **Restrict Admin Privileges** – Only assign **Jira Admin** access to **essential personnel**.

2. **Use Group-Based Permissions** – Instead of assigning individual permissions, use **Jira user groups** (e.g., `Developers`, `QA`, `Managers`).
3. **Audit User Access Regularly** – Remove **inactive users** and review **permission schemes** every **quarter**.

🚀 **Result:** Reduced risk of **accidental changes or security breaches**.

2.2. Enforce Secure Jira Hosting and Deployment Settings

🔍 **For Jira Cloud Users:**
✔ Enable **IP Allowlisting** to restrict access to specific locations.
✔ Configure **Audit Logs** to track **all administrative changes**.

🔍 **For Jira Server / Data Center Users:**
✔ Enable **HTTPS with SSL/TLS encryption** for secure access.
✔ Restrict **database access** using **firewall rules**.
✔ Configure **Jira application logs** to detect anomalies.

🚀 **Result:** Enhanced **data security and compliance** with security best practices.

2.3. Secure Jira Integrations and Marketplace Apps

🔍 **Risk:**
✔ Some **third-party Jira apps** may have **security vulnerabilities**.
✔ Unsecured integrations can **leak confidential data** to external services.

🔧 **Solution:**
✔ **Only install trusted apps** from the **Atlassian Marketplace**.
✔ Review app **security settings** and limit **data-sharing permissions**.
✔ Regularly **update all installed plugins** to patch known vulnerabilities.

⬛ **Best Practice:** Conduct **annual security reviews** of all Jira integrations.

2.4. Monitor and Log Jira Security Events

🔍 **Key Security Events to Track in Jira Logs:**
✔ **Failed login attempts** (Brute-force attack detection)
✔ **Unauthorized API access attempts**
✔ **Permission changes** (Detecting privilege escalation attacks)
✔ **Data export events** (Preventing insider threats)

🔧 **How to Enable Security Logging in Jira:**

1. Navigate to **Jira Administration → System → Logging and Profiling**.
2. Enable **Advanced Logging** for authentication and access control events.
3. Set up **SIEM (Security Information and Event Management) integration** for real-time monitoring.

🚀 **Result:** Improved **threat detection and incident response**.

2.5. Secure Jira Data with Encryption and Compliance Measures

🔍 **Compliance Risks:**
✔ Jira stores sensitive development data that **must be encrypted**.
✔ Some companies **must comply** with GDPR, HIPAA, or ISO 27001 standards.

🔧 **Solution:**
✔ Enable **data encryption at rest** (for Jira Server users, use **encrypted disk storage**).
✔ Use **Atlassian Access** for centralized security and compliance.
✔ Conduct **annual security audits** for **regulatory compliance**.

🚀 **Result:** Protection against **data breaches and regulatory fines**.

3. Best Practices Checklist for Jira Security

Security Measure	Action Required
Enable Multi-Factor Authentication (MFA)	■ Required for all users
Limit Admin Privileges	■ Only essential team members
Enforce Strong Password Policies	■ Use complex passwords & rotation
Restrict API Access	■ Use OAuth2 and IP restrictions
Secure Jira Workflows	■ Limit issue transitions
Regular Backup & Disaster Recovery	■ Schedule daily backups
Monitor Security Logs	■ Detect and respond to threats
Audit User Permissions Quarterly	■ Remove inactive users
Use HTTPS Encryption	■ Secure Jira traffic

Conclusion

By following **these security best practices**, development teams can:

✔ **Protect Jira data from unauthorized access and cyber threats**
✔ **Ensure compliance with security and privacy regulations**
✔ **Monitor and detect security risks in real-time**
✔ **Securely manage Jira integrations, workflows, and API access**

With the right **security measures in place**, Jira remains a **safe, scalable, and resilient** tool for software development teams.

Scaling Jira as Your Team Grows

As development teams **expand** and projects become **more complex**, Jira must be **scaled** to accommodate more **users, workflows, and data**. Without **proper scaling strategies**, Jira can suffer from **performance bottlenecks, permission conflicts, and inefficient workflows**, leading to **delays, frustration, and mismanagement**.

Scaling Jira effectively ensures:

■ **Fast and efficient performance for large teams**
■ **Seamless collaboration across multiple teams and departments**
■ **Proper permission management to prevent security risks**
■ **Optimized workflows to handle increasing project complexity**

In this chapter, we'll cover:

- **Challenges of scaling Jira in growing teams**
- **Best practices for scaling Jira's infrastructure and workflows**
- **Managing users, permissions, and security at scale**
- **Optimizing Jira for multi-team and enterprise-level use**

By the end, you'll be equipped with the strategies needed to **keep Jira running smoothly, even as your team and projects grow**.

---

1. Common Challenges of Scaling Jira

1.1. Performance Issues as User Count Increases

🔔 **Problem:**
✔ Jira becomes **slower** as more users and issues are added.
✔ Dashboards and filters **take longer to load** due to **large datasets**.
✔ **JQL queries and reports** run inefficiently.

🛠 **Solution:**
✔ Archive **old issues** to **reduce database load**.
✔ Optimize **JQL queries** to use **indexed fields**.
✔ Use **Jira Data Center** for high-availability and load balancing.

■ **Best Practice:** Monitor **Jira system logs** to detect slow-performing queries and optimize indexing.

1.2. Managing Multiple Teams and Projects Efficiently

🔔 **Problem:**
✔ Different teams need **custom workflows, boards, and permissions**, leading to **management complexity**.
✔ Overlapping projects cause **visibility and accountability issues**.

🛠 **Solution:**
✔ Use **Jira Portfolio Management** tools like **Advanced Roadmaps**.
✔ Implement **standardized workflows** to maintain consistency.
✔ Create **separate Jira boards per team** but allow cross-team collaboration via shared dashboards.

■ **Best Practice:** Use **Jira Components** and **Epics** to organize work across teams.

1.3. User and Permission Management at Scale

▲ **Problem:**
✔ Too many users with **admin privileges** increase **security risks**.
✔ Teams struggle to **find the right people** for issue assignments.
✔ Permissions are **inconsistent across projects**, causing **access issues**.

✗ **Solution:**
✔ Implement **Group-Based Permissions** instead of assigning roles individually.
✔ Limit **Admin Access** to essential users only.
✔ Use **User Directories (LDAP, SAML, Single Sign-On)** to sync and manage access.

■ **Best Practice:** Review and audit **user permissions quarterly** to remove inactive users.

1.4. Scaling Jira Workflows Without Causing Bottlenecks

▲ **Problem:**
✔ Complex workflows **slow down issue transitions**.
✔ Overuse of **validators, conditions, and post-functions** adds **delays**.
✔ Automation rules cause **workflow conflicts**.

✗ **Solution:**
✔ **Simplify workflows** by reducing unnecessary transition steps.
✔ Use **automation sparingly** and **monitor execution logs**.
✔ Implement **parallel workflows** for different teams instead of forcing a single complex workflow.

■ **Best Practice:** **Test new workflows in a sandbox environment** before applying them to production.

---

2. Best Practices for Scaling Jira Infrastructure

2.1. Scaling Jira Cloud vs. Jira Data Center

Jira Cloud (Recommended for fast-growing teams):
✔ Auto-scales with **Atlassian-hosted infrastructure**.
✔ Best for **distributed teams that don't want infrastructure management**.
✔ Limited customization but **easy to maintain**.

Jira Data Center (Recommended for enterprises):
✔ Provides **load balancing and failover support**.
✔ Can handle **thousands of concurrent users**.
✔ Requires **on-premise infrastructure management**.

■ **Best Practice:** If scaling **beyond 500 users**, consider moving to **Jira Data Center**.

2.2. Optimizing Jira for High Performance

✔ **Archive or Delete Old Issues** – Reduces **database load and search time**.
✔ **Limit Custom Fields** – Too many custom fields **slow down issue creation**.
✔ **Use Content Delivery Networks (CDN)** – Improves **global access speed**.
✔ **Optimize Dashboard Gadgets** – Avoid **heavy widgets** that slow down load times.

▪ **Best Practice:** Set up **Performance Monitoring Tools** like Jira Performance Testing Toolkit.

2.3. Managing Large-Scale Backlogs Efficiently

🔔 **Problem:**
✔ Large backlogs make **prioritization and sprint planning difficult**.
✔ Searching and filtering **becomes slow** with thousands of issues.

🔧 **Solution:**
✔ Implement **Backlog Grooming Practices** – **Close stale issues** older than 6 months.
✔ Use **JQL Smart Filters** to segment and manage large backlogs.
✔ Prioritize work using **Epics, Labels, and Components**.

▪ **Best Practice:** Run a **monthly backlog review** to remove or merge outdated issues.

2.4. Automating and Standardizing Processes at Scale

🔔 **Problem:**
✔ Scaling teams often create **inconsistent workflows** across projects.
✔ **Manual task management** slows down **large development teams**.

🔧 **Solution:**
✔ Use **Jira Automation Rules** to assign tasks based on issue type.
✔ Standardize **Project Templates** for onboarding new teams.
✔ Create **Global Workflows** that multiple teams can reuse.

▪ **Best Practice:** Store **best practices and templates** in Jira Confluence for team consistency.

2.5. Security and Compliance Considerations at Scale

🔔 **Problem:**
✔ More users increase **security risks**.
✔ Teams need to **comply with GDPR, ISO, or HIPAA standards**.

🔧 **Solution:**
✔ Implement **Role-Based Access Control (RBAC)** for permissions.
✔ Enable **audit logs** to track admin changes and user access.
✔ Encrypt **Jira data at rest and in transit** for compliance.

▪ **Best Practice:** Conduct **annual security audits** to review compliance measures.

---

3. Checklist for Scaling Jira

Category	Scaling Strategy
Performance	Archive old issues, optimize JQL queries, limit dashboard gadgets
User Management	Use group-based permissions, audit roles quarterly, integrate SSO
Workflow Optimization	Simplify transitions, use automation sparingly, standardize templates
Infrastructure Scaling	Use Jira Cloud for auto-scaling, Jira Data Center for enterprise needs
Security	Enable RBAC, encrypt data, enable audit logs
Backlog Management	Use backlog grooming, smart filters, and epic prioritization

Conclusion

By implementing **scalable Jira strategies**, teams can:

✔ Ensure **fast performance, even with thousands of users**.
✔ Manage **multiple teams and projects efficiently**.
✔ Maintain **security and compliance as the organization grows**.
✔ Optimize **backlog management, workflows, and automation** for large-scale projects.

With the **right scaling approach**, Jira remains an **efficient, secure, and high-performing tool**, no matter how large your development team grows.

Part 8:
Real-World Case Studies

Case Study: Streamlining a DevOps Pipeline with Jira

A well-optimized **DevOps pipeline** enables faster software releases, improved collaboration, and enhanced **CI/CD (Continuous Integration/Continuous Deployment) workflows**. However, many teams struggle with **fragmented toolchains, inefficient issue tracking, and lack of visibility into deployments**.

In this case study, we'll explore how **a mid-sized software company** streamlined its DevOps pipeline using **Jira, Bitbucket, and Jenkins**, reducing deployment times by **30%** and improving **collaboration between developers, testers, and operations teams**.

1. Background

Company: TechX Solutions (Pseudonym)
Industry: SaaS (Software as a Service)
Team Size: 100+ developers, QA, and DevOps engineers
Tech Stack: AWS, Kubernetes, Jenkins, Git, Jira, Bitbucket

Challenges Faced Before Jira Optimization:
✔ **Lack of visibility** into development, testing, and deployment stages.
✔ **Slow release cycles** due to inefficient handoffs between dev and ops teams.
✔ **Manual tracking of builds and deployments** leading to errors.
✔ **Disorganized backlog** with poorly prioritized issues and unstructured sprints.

To address these issues, TechX Solutions integrated **Jira with their DevOps pipeline**, automating workflows, optimizing CI/CD processes, and improving cross-team collaboration.

2. Challenges and Problems Before Jira Integration

2.1. Fragmented Development and Operations Teams

🔒 **Problem:**
✔ Developers, testers, and operations teams worked in **separate silos**, leading to **miscommunication and delays**.
✔ Issues were **logged manually** across different systems (Slack, spreadsheets, email).

🔧 **Solution:**
✔ Unified all teams under **Jira with a DevOps-focused workflow**, ensuring visibility from issue creation to production deployment.

✔ Set up **Jira dashboards** displaying real-time **CI/CD pipeline status**, build failures, and release progress.

■ **Result:** Reduced **hand-off time** between dev, QA, and ops teams by **40%**.

2.2. Slow and Error-Prone Deployments

🔺 **Problem:**
✔ Deployments were **initiated manually**, increasing human error.
✔ There was **no automated rollback mechanism** in case of failures.
✔ Deployment status **was not linked to Jira**, making tracking difficult.

🛠 **Solution:**
✔ Integrated **Jira with Jenkins** to trigger **automated deployments** directly from Jira tickets.
✔ Configured **Jira Automation** to update issue status when builds pass or fail.
✔ Set up **auto-rollback scripts** triggered upon failed deployments.

■ **Result:** Deployment failures reduced by **50%**, and rollback processes were fully automated.

2.3. Unstructured Sprint and Issue Management

🔺 **Problem:**
✔ Sprint backlogs contained **unprioritized tasks**, leading to **development bottlenecks**.
✔ Issues were often **missing acceptance criteria**, causing rework and delayed releases.

🛠 **Solution:**
✔ Implemented **Jira Scrum Boards** to structure **sprints with clear priorities**.
✔ Enforced **Definition of Ready (DoR) and Definition of Done (DoD)** before moving tasks to the next stage.
✔ Used **Jira Advanced Roadmaps** to align development priorities with DevOps goals.

■ **Result:** Sprint completion rates increased by **25%**, and rework due to incomplete stories was reduced.

---

3. Jira Integration with DevOps Tools

To fully streamline the DevOps pipeline, TechX Solutions integrated Jira with:

3.1. Bitbucket for Version Control

■ **Jira and Bitbucket integration** enabled:
✔ Automatic linking of **Git branches, commits, and pull requests** to Jira tickets.
✔ Developers to **transition Jira issues by merging pull requests** (e.g., moving an issue to "In Review" upon PR creation).
✔ **Automated code reviews** triggered within Jira workflows.

🚀 **Result:** Reduced manual tracking of branches and code reviews by **30%**.

3.2. Jenkins for Continuous Integration & Deployment

■ **Jira and Jenkins integration** enabled:
✔ Builds and deployments to be **tracked inside Jira** via automation rules.
✔ **Build failures** to automatically create Jira issues, notifying the appropriate teams.
✔ Release notes to be **auto-generated** in Jira from successful builds.

🚀 **Result:** Deployment coordination improved by **35%**, and release failures were proactively addressed.

3.3. Confluence for Documentation and Change Management

■ **Jira and Confluence integration** enabled:
✔ Automatic **documentation updates** when new features were deployed.
✔ Jira issues linked directly to **release notes and sprint retrospectives**.

🚀 **Result:** Reduced time spent on **manual documentation updates by 40%**.

---

4. Workflow Automation in Jira

To further streamline DevOps processes, TechX Solutions implemented **Jira Automation Rules** for:

Automation Rule	Outcome
Auto-assign new tickets based on labels (bug, feature, task)	Ensured the right team member got the issue immediately
Move tickets automatically from "To Do" to "In Progress" when a branch is created	Removed manual updates and improved tracking
Trigger CI/CD builds when an issue is moved to "Ready for Deployment"	Automated the pipeline, reducing manual deployment steps
Close issues automatically when PRs are merged	Ensured work was reflected accurately in Jira

■ **Result:** Manual tracking efforts **dropped by 60%**, allowing engineers to focus on development.

---

5. Key Results After Implementing Jira for DevOps

■ **Metrics Before vs. After Jira DevOps Integration**

Metric	Before	After Jira Optimization	Improvement
Deployment Frequency	Once every **2 weeks**	Twice a week	🚀 **4x faster releases**
Rollback Time	**4 hours** per failed deploy	**Automated rollback in 5 min**	⏳ **96% faster recovery**
Sprint Completion Rate	**65% of planned issues completed**	**90%+ sprint completion**	■ **25% increase in dev efficiency**

Manual Issue Tracking Time	2 hours per week per engineer	30 minutes per week	⏳ 75% reduction
Deployment Failure Rate	20% of deployments failed	10% failure rate	⚡ 50% reduction in failed deploys

6. Lessons Learned

■ **Standardizing workflows across Dev, QA, and Ops teams was crucial** – Without a unified Jira workflow, cross-team collaboration was chaotic.

■ **Automating repetitive tasks freed up developer time** – Manual issue tracking and status updates slowed productivity before automation was in place.

■ **Real-time visibility into DevOps status improved decision-making** – Linking Jira with Jenkins, Bitbucket, and dashboards allowed teams to quickly identify and fix issues.

■ **Small, frequent deployments led to higher stability** – Instead of massive bi-weekly releases, shorter release cycles ensured faster bug detection and resolution.

Conclusion

By **integrating Jira with DevOps tools**, TechX Solutions transformed their software delivery process. The combination of **automated workflows, CI/CD integration, and structured sprint planning** led to:

✔ **30% faster development cycles**
✔ **50% fewer failed deployments**
✔ **Improved visibility across teams**
✔ **Less time spent on manual tracking**

For any development team **looking to optimize their DevOps pipeline**, Jira **provides a central hub** for tracking, automating, and scaling CI/CD workflows efficiently.

Case Study: Agile Transformation in a SaaS Startup

Agile methodologies have revolutionized software development, especially in **fast-growing SaaS (Software-as-a-Service) startups**, where speed, flexibility, and adaptability are key to success. However, many startups struggle to **scale Agile effectively**, facing challenges such as **unstructured workflows, poor backlog management, and misalignment between development and business goals**.

In this case study, we'll explore how a SaaS startup, **CloudFlow Inc.** (pseudonym), successfully transitioned from **ad-hoc development to a structured Agile framework** using **Jira**. By implementing **Agile workflows, sprint planning, backlog management, and automation**, CloudFlow:

■ Increased sprint completion rates by 35%
■ Reduced development cycle time from 4 weeks to 2 weeks
■ Improved collaboration between development, product, and customer support teams

This chapter will provide a **step-by-step breakdown** of how the startup achieved this Agile transformation using **Jira as the backbone of their development process**.

---

1. Background

Company Profile

- **Company:** CloudFlow Inc. (Pseudonym)
- **Industry:** SaaS (Cloud-based workflow automation software)
- **Team Size:** 50+ engineers, designers, product managers, and QA specialists
- **Development Model:** Transitioning from **ad-hoc development** to **Agile Scrum**
- **Challenges:** Slow release cycles, unstructured backlog, lack of cross-team visibility

Challenges Faced Before Agile Implementation

🔔 **Key Problems Identified:**
✔ **Lack of a structured development process** → Features were built reactively with no clear roadmap.
✔ **No centralized backlog management** → Developers worked on tasks without clear prioritization.
✔ **Ineffective sprint planning** → Sprints often exceeded timelines due to **scope creep**.
✔ **Poor cross-functional collaboration** → Misalignment between developers, QA, and product managers.
✔ **Manual issue tracking** → Tasks were managed through Slack and spreadsheets, leading to lost tickets.

To address these problems, CloudFlow decided to **fully integrate Agile methodologies with Jira**, improving **sprint planning, backlog management, and cross-functional team coordination**.

---

2. Agile Transformation Using Jira

2.1. Implementing Scrum in Jira

Before:

- No structured sprint planning or backlog grooming.
- Issues tracked via spreadsheets and Slack conversations.
- Developers worked on features **without clear acceptance criteria**.

After:

- Adopted **Scrum methodology** with **2-week sprints**.
- Used **Jira Scrum Boards** for backlog refinement, sprint planning, and tracking progress.
- Enforced **Definition of Ready (DoR) and Definition of Done (DoD)** for each story.

■ **Results:** Sprint success rate improved from **55% to 90%**, reducing carry-over work.

2.2. Centralizing and Structuring the Backlog

Before:

- Backlog had **hundreds of unorganized issues**, making prioritization difficult.
- No distinction between **feature requests, bugs, and technical debt**.
- Teams worked on **low-priority tasks** instead of mission-critical features.

After:

- Created **separate Jira Issue Types** for:
  - **Stories (New Features)**
  - **Bugs (Defects & Hotfixes)**
  - **Technical Debt (Refactoring & Performance Improvements)**
- Used **Epics and Labels** to categorize backlog items.
- Prioritized issues using **MoSCoW (Must-have, Should-have, Could-have, Won't-have) method**.

■ **Results:** Product managers and developers aligned on **feature prioritization**, reducing miscommunication.

2.3. Structuring Sprint Planning in Jira

Before:

- Sprints often exceeded planned timeframes.
- Stories were added mid-sprint, causing **scope creep**.
- No visibility into **workload distribution** among developers.

After:

- Implemented **Jira Workload Management** to evenly distribute tasks.
- Used **Sprint Goals** to define **clear objectives** before each sprint.
- Enforced a **Sprint Freeze Policy** (No new stories added once sprint starts).
- Used **Story Points for estimation** and **Velocity Charts** for predictability.

■ **Results:** Sprint predictability improved, reducing **missed deadlines by 40%**.

2.4. Improving Cross-Team Collaboration

Before:

- Developers, designers, and QA teams worked in silos.
- Product Managers struggled to get updates from engineering.
- Customer support teams had no insight into **bug fixes and feature releases**.

After:

- Integrated **Jira with Slack and Confluence** for real-time communication.
- Linked Jira **bug reports** with customer support tickets from Zendesk.
- Conducted **Sprint Retrospectives** using Jira Confluence for continuous improvement.

■ **Results:** Improved communication between **engineering, product, and support teams**, reducing feature release delays.

2.5. Automating Agile Workflows with Jira

To further **reduce manual effort**, CloudFlow implemented **Jira Automation Rules** for:

Automation Rule	Outcome
Automatically transition issues **to "In Progress" when assigned**	Eliminated manual status updates
Send Slack notifications when a **critical bug is reported**	Improved DevOps responsiveness
Auto-close issues that are **inactive for 30 days**	Kept the backlog clean
Trigger CI/CD pipeline **when an issue moves to "Ready for Deployment"**	Automated deployment tracking

■ **Results:** Manual issue tracking efforts reduced by **50%**, allowing developers to focus on coding.

---

3. Measuring the Impact of Agile Transformation

■ **Key Metrics Before vs. After Agile Implementation**

Metric	Before Agile	After Agile with Jira	Improvement
Sprint Completion Rate	55%	90%	🚀 35% increase
Average Development Cycle Time	4 weeks	2 weeks	🔥 50% faster releases
Scope Creep (Unplanned Work Added)	30% per sprint	5% per sprint	⚡ 83% reduction
Customer Bug Resolution Time	7 days	3 days	🛠 57% faster bug fixes
Cross-Team Collaboration Score (Survey)	6/10	9/10	■ 50% improvement

4. Lessons Learned

■ **1. A structured backlog improves efficiency** – Without proper **issue categorization and prioritization**, teams waste time on low-impact tasks.

■ **2. Sprint planning must be disciplined** – Enforcing a **Sprint Freeze Policy** prevented teams from overloading themselves mid-sprint.

■ **3. Automation eliminates unnecessary manual work** – Automating repetitive Jira tasks saved **developer hours every sprint**.

■ **4. Cross-functional collaboration is key to Agile success** – When **developers, QA, and product teams work in sync**, releases happen faster.

Conclusion

By **adopting Jira for Agile project management**, CloudFlow Inc. transformed their **development process**, leading to:

✔ **35% improvement in sprint success rate**
✔ **50% faster development cycles**
✔ **Better backlog organization and prioritization**
✔ **Reduced scope creep and improved cross-team collaboration**

For any **SaaS startup looking to scale Agile**, Jira provides the **tools and structure** needed to optimize **workflows, sprint planning, and backlog management**.

Part 9:
Future-Proofing Your Jira Setup

Adapting Jira for AI-Driven Development

As software development evolves, **Artificial Intelligence (AI) and Machine Learning (ML)** are becoming central to **automating workflows, predicting issues, and optimizing team productivity**. AI-driven development is no longer a futuristic concept—it's happening now, with tools that enhance **issue tracking, sprint planning, and CI/CD pipelines**.

Jira, as a leading Agile project management tool, is **rapidly integrating AI-powered features** to help development teams:

- **Predict bottlenecks** and optimize sprint planning.
- **Automate repetitive tasks** with AI-driven workflows.
- **Enhance issue resolution** with intelligent recommendations.
- **Improve code quality** with AI-assisted reviews.

This chapter explores how teams can **leverage AI to enhance Jira workflows, automate project management, and streamline software development**.

1. The Role of AI in Modern Software Development

AI is transforming the way teams develop, test, and deploy software. Here's how AI-driven development is shaping Jira usage:

1.1. AI-Powered Agile Project Management

- AI can analyze past sprint data to **predict delays and suggest task reallocation**.
- Machine learning models identify **team velocity patterns** and **optimize workload distribution**.
- AI-driven insights **reduce sprint overruns** by flagging potential blockers before they cause delays.

1.2. AI-Enhanced Bug Tracking and Issue Resolution

- AI automatically categorizes **incoming issues as bugs, features, or technical debt**.
- NLP (Natural Language Processing) models help Jira **analyze bug reports** and suggest similar historical tickets.
- AI-powered chatbots assist developers in **resolving Jira issues faster** by providing relevant documentation and fixes.

1.3. Intelligent Workflow Automation

- AI predicts when issues **should be escalated** based on past resolution times.
- AI-powered automation rules auto-assign **high-priority bugs to the right developers**.
- Smart suggestions for **optimal sprint backlog prioritization** based on historical completion rates.

Outcome: AI enables teams to make **data-driven decisions** and **eliminate inefficiencies** in software development.

2. AI-Driven Jira Features and Integrations

Jira is already incorporating **AI-powered tools and integrations** to streamline development processes.

2.1. AI-Powered Predictive Issue Management

🚀 **Feature:** AI-driven **predictive analytics** in Jira can:
✔ Forecast **which tasks are likely to exceed sprint deadlines**.
✔ Identify **at-risk issues** based on past project delays.
✔ Suggest backlog grooming improvements based on historical trends.

🔧 **How to Implement in Jira:**
✔ Use **Jira Advanced Roadmaps + AI analytics tools (e.g., Atlassian Intelligence)** for predictive sprint management.
✔ Leverage **AI-powered backlog prioritization** with tools like **Automation for Jira**.

⬛ **Impact:** Teams **reduce sprint failures** and **optimize backlog prioritization**.

2.2. AI for Code Quality and Automated Code Reviews

🚀 **Feature:** AI tools now **analyze pull requests and provide feedback** on code quality, security, and maintainability.

🔧 **How to Implement in Jira:**
✔ Integrate Jira with **GitHub Copilot, Codacy, or DeepCode** for AI-assisted code reviews.
✔ Use **Bitbucket Pipelines + AI-powered static code analysis tools** to detect security vulnerabilities automatically.
✔ Link Jira issues to AI-driven **automated test coverage reports**.

⬛ **Impact:** Reduces **code review time by 30%** and **improves code maintainability**.

2.3. AI-Powered Jira Automation

🚀 **Feature:** AI-powered automation can:
✔ Automatically **categorize issues** based on content and severity.
✔ Assign issues to **developers best suited for the task** based on past work.
✔ Suggest **resolution steps based on historical fixes** for similar issues.

🔧 **How to Implement in Jira:**
✔ Use **Jira Automation Rules + Atlassian Intelligence** for smart issue categorization.
✔ Connect Jira with **AI-driven chatbots (e.g., Atlassian Assist, Slack AI bots)** for automated ticket triage.

⬛ **Impact:** Eliminates **manual task assignment** and **reduces time spent on issue categorization**.

2.4. AI-Powered Virtual Assistants for Jira

🚀 **Feature:** AI-powered virtual assistants can:
✔ Answer **Jira-related queries** using Natural Language Processing (NLP).

✔ Automate **ticket updates, status changes, and comments** using voice commands.
✔ Provide **real-time sprint insights** through AI-driven dashboards.

🔧 **How to Implement in Jira:**
✔ Integrate Jira with **Atlassian Intelligence, ChatGPT, or Microsoft Copilot** for conversational AI support.
✔ Use **voice-enabled Jira bots (e.g., Alexa for Jira, Jira Slack AI bots)** to interact with issues hands-free.

⬛ **Impact:** Saves **developer time** by **automating Jira interactions**.

3. Real-World Use Cases of AI in Jira

📌 **Case Study 1: AI-Powered Sprint Planning**
A fintech startup **integrated AI into Jira to predict sprint completion rates**. By analyzing past velocity, AI suggested **better backlog prioritization**, increasing sprint efficiency by **40%**.

📌 **Case Study 2: AI for Bug Triage in a SaaS Company**
A SaaS company used **AI-powered bug categorization in Jira** to **reduce triage time from 4 hours to 30 minutes** per sprint. AI assigned bugs automatically based on **historical resolution data**.

📌 **Case Study 3: AI-Driven Code Review Integration**
An enterprise tech firm **automated code reviews in Jira** using **Bitbucket AI**. This **reduced code review delays by 35%** while improving overall code quality.

4. Preparing Your Jira Setup for AI-Driven Development

4.1. Key Steps to Implement AI in Jira

Step	Action Item
Step 1: Identify AI Use Cases	Determine where AI can automate **issue tracking, backlog prioritization, or sprint planning**.
Step 2: Integrate AI-Powered Tools	Use **Jira Automation, Atlassian Intelligence, and AI-powered Git tools**.
Step 3: Optimize Workflows with AI	Implement **smart Jira Automation Rules** for issue management.
Step 4: Train AI Models with Historical Data	AI tools **improve over time** by learning from past Jira issues.
Step 5: Continuously Monitor AI Performance	Track **AI recommendations and adjust automation rules as needed**.

⬛ **Best Practice:** Regularly evaluate **AI-generated insights** to ensure they align with team workflows.

5. Challenges and Considerations for AI in Jira

🔔 1. AI Bias in Issue Prioritization

- AI may **over-prioritize certain types of issues** based on past trends.
- Solution: Regularly **review AI-based recommendations** to avoid **algorithmic bias**.

🔔 2. Security & Data Privacy Concerns

- AI tools require **access to Jira issue data**, which may contain sensitive information.
- Solution: Use **AI-powered Jira apps with enterprise-grade security compliance**.

🔔 3. Resistance to AI Adoption

- Some teams may be hesitant to **fully automate Jira processes**.
- Solution: Gradually introduce **AI enhancements alongside manual workflows**.

Conclusion

AI is transforming **how teams manage software development in Jira**, from **predictive issue tracking** to **intelligent backlog prioritization** and **automated code reviews**. By **integrating AI-powered automation, chatbots, and predictive analytics**, teams can:

✔ **Accelerate sprint planning and backlog grooming**
✔ **Reduce manual issue tracking and task assignment**
✔ **Enhance code quality with AI-driven code reviews**
✔ **Improve team efficiency with AI-powered automation**

As AI continues to evolve, **Jira will become an even more powerful tool for Agile and DevOps teams**.

Preparing for Jira's Evolution: Cloud-First Trends

The software industry is rapidly moving toward **cloud-native development**, and **Jira is at the forefront of this transition**. Atlassian has announced a **cloud-first strategy**, with **Jira Cloud receiving priority updates** while **Jira Server has been officially discontinued**.

For development teams relying on **Jira for Agile project management**, it's crucial to **adapt to cloud-first trends**, ensuring that Jira continues to serve as an effective collaboration and workflow automation tool.

This chapter will explore:

■ The **key trends driving Jira's cloud-first evolution.**
■ The **benefits of moving to Jira Cloud vs. Jira Data Center.**
■ Best practices for **preparing development teams for Jira's future.**
■ How to **leverage new cloud-native Jira features.**

1. Why Jira Is Moving to a Cloud-First Model

Atlassian's **cloud-first approach** is a response to **market demands for scalability, automation, and AI-powered capabilities**. Here's why Jira Cloud is the future:

1.1. End of Jira Server and Shift to Cloud

- **Jira Server support ended in 2024,** forcing teams to migrate to **Jira Cloud or Data Center.**
- **New features and updates** are now **exclusive to Jira Cloud,** with Atlassian focusing on **SaaS-first solutions.**

1.2. Cloud Adoption for Scalability and Performance

- **Jira Cloud provides automatic scaling,** eliminating **manual infrastructure management.**
- **Atlassian-hosted SaaS solutions** offer **built-in security, compliance, and updates.**

1.3. AI and Automation-Driven Features in Jira Cloud

- **AI-powered issue recommendations and sprint planning** are exclusive to Jira Cloud.
- **Cloud-first automation tools** simplify repetitive Jira tasks, increasing development efficiency.

🚀 **Impact:** Development teams that migrate to Jira Cloud **benefit from continuous innovation and reduced maintenance overhead.**

2. Jira Cloud vs. Jira Data Center: Choosing the Right Path

As teams transition away from Jira Server, they must choose between:

■ **Jira Cloud:** A fully **managed SaaS solution**, ideal for **fast-moving Agile teams.**
■ **Jira Data Center:** A **self-hosted enterprise solution**, designed for **regulated industries requiring data control.**

2.1. Comparison: Jira Cloud vs. Jira Data Center

Feature	Jira Cloud	Jira Data Center

Hosting	Atlassian-managed SaaS	Self-hosted (on-premises or AWS/Azure)
Maintenance	Fully managed	Requires infrastructure & IT support
AI and Automation Features	■ Yes (exclusive AI-powered capabilities)	✕ Limited
Scalability	■ Automatic	✕ Manual
Security & Compliance	■ SOC2, GDPR, HIPAA-ready	■ More control over security
Customization & Marketplace Apps	■ Available, but **some apps are cloud-only**	■ More control over custom plugins
Performance Optimization	■ Automatically optimized	✕ Requires manual tuning
Best For	Agile teams, startups, and mid-size enterprises	Large enterprises needing full control

🚀 **Recommendation:**

- If **your team prioritizes ease of use, automation, and AI features** → **Jira Cloud is the best choice**.
- If **your organization requires on-premise control and strict compliance** → **Jira Data Center is the alternative**.

---

3. Key Cloud-First Trends Shaping Jira's Future

Jira's cloud evolution is driven by **several major trends** impacting software development teams:

3.1. AI and Machine Learning in Jira Cloud

- **AI-powered backlog prioritization** recommends the next best tasks based on historical performance.
- **Automated issue categorization** reduces manual ticket triage.
- **Predictive sprint planning** estimates workload and sprint capacity.

🚀 **What Teams Can Do:**

- Start **experimenting with Jira AI-powered features** for smarter project tracking.

3.2. No-Code & Low-Code Jira Customizations

- **No-code automation tools** enable teams to build workflows **without scripting**.
- Jira Cloud's **Automation for Jira** lets users create rules for **automated issue tracking, sprint transitions, and CI/CD integration**.

🚀 **What Teams Can Do:**

- Explore **Jira Automation Rules** to reduce repetitive work and streamline workflows.

3.3. Integration with DevOps & Cloud-Native CI/CD Pipelines

- **Jira Cloud natively integrates with GitHub Actions, Bitbucket Pipelines, and Jenkins.**
- **Real-time deployment tracking in Jira** links pull requests to user stories and releases.

🚀 **What Teams Can Do:**

- Connect **Jira Cloud to CI/CD pipelines** for **automated deployment tracking**.

3.4. Increased Security & Compliance in Cloud Environments

- Atlassian has **strengthened security measures in Jira Cloud**, including:
  - ✔ **SSO (Single Sign-On)** with OAuth and SAML.
  - ✔ **Data residency options** for GDPR compliance.
  - ✔ **Audit logs and advanced permissions** for enterprise users.

🚀 **What Teams Can Do:**

- Enable **Jira Cloud security best practices** (2FA, role-based access controls).

3.5. Improved Performance & Scalability

- **Jira Cloud scales dynamically**, removing the need for **manual database tuning or server optimization**.
- **Performance enhancements** include **faster queries, async processing, and smart caching**.

🚀 **What Teams Can Do:**

- **Migrate to Jira Cloud for automatic performance tuning** instead of maintaining on-premise servers.

4. Best Practices for Preparing for Jira's Cloud-First Future

To **future-proof** your Jira setup, follow these best practices:

4.1. Plan Your Migration to Jira Cloud

- Evaluate your **existing Jira Server setup**.
- Use **Atlassian's Cloud Migration Assistant** for a smooth transition.
- Test integrations before fully switching to Jira Cloud.

4.2. Leverage AI & Automation in Jira Cloud

- Explore **AI-powered backlog recommendations** for better sprint planning.
- Use **Jira Automation Rules** to eliminate repetitive tasks.

4.3. Optimize Jira for DevOps & CI/CD

- Integrate **Jira Cloud with GitHub, Bitbucket, and Jenkins**.
- Enable **real-time deployment tracking** for visibility into production releases.

4.4. Strengthen Jira Cloud Security & Compliance

- Enable **SAML SSO, 2FA, and data encryption**.
- Set up **role-based access controls** for sensitive project data.

4.5. Train Teams on Cloud-First Jira Best Practices

- Educate teams on **new Jira Cloud features**.
- Encourage the use of **Jira AI recommendations** for issue prioritization.

---

5. Conclusion

Jira's transition to a **cloud-first ecosystem** presents an opportunity for **development teams to enhance efficiency, automation, and security**.

By embracing **Jira Cloud and its AI-powered capabilities**, teams can:

✔ **Future-proof project management workflows**.
✔ **Automate repetitive tasks with AI and no-code tools**.
✔ **Optimize CI/CD pipelines and DevOps integrations**.
✔ **Benefit from continuous performance and security updates**.

As **Atlassian continues to invest in cloud-based innovation, early adoption of Jira Cloud ensures teams stay ahead in the evolving Agile and DevOps landscape**.

🚀 **Next Steps:** If your team is still on Jira Server, begin planning **your migration to Jira Cloud** today!

Appendices

Appendix A: Jira Query Language (JQL) Cheat Sheet

Jira Query Language (JQL) is **a powerful way to search and filter issues in Jira**. Whether you need to **track project progress, find unresolved bugs, or analyze sprint performance**, JQL allows **advanced queries** that go beyond Jira's basic search filters.

This **JQL Cheat Sheet** provides:
■ **Basic syntax and structure** of JQL queries.
■ **Common JQL operators and functions**.
■ **Advanced query techniques** for Agile and DevOps teams.
■ **Examples for real-world use cases**.

---

1. Basic JQL Syntax

A JQL query consists of **fields, operators, and values**, structured as:

```
Field Operator Value
```

Example:

```
status = "In Progress"
```

📌 This query **finds all issues that are currently in progress**.

---

2. Common JQL Fields

JQL fields represent **issue attributes**. Below are commonly used fields:

Field	Description	Example Query
project	Filters by project name or key	`project = "Mobile App"`
status	Filters by issue status	`status = "To Do"`
assignee	Finds issues assigned to a user	`assignee = "john.doe"`
reporter	Finds issues reported by a user	`reporter = "alice.smith"`
priority	Filters by issue priority	`priority = High`
type	Filters by issue type (Bug, Story, Task)	`type = Bug`

labels	Finds issues with specific labels	`labels = "frontend"`
resolution	Filters by resolution status	`resolution = Unresolved`
sprint	Finds issues in a specific sprint	`sprint = "Sprint 5"`
fixVersion	Filters issues by release version	`fixVersion = "v2.0"`

3. JQL Operators

JQL supports various **operators** for **filtering and comparing data**.

Operator	Description	Example Query
`=`	Equals	`status = "Done"`
`!=`	Not equal to	`status != "Closed"`
`>`	Greater than	`priority > Medium`
`<`	Less than	`priority < High`
`>=`	Greater than or equal to	`created >= "2023-01-01"`
`<=`	Less than or equal to	`duedate <= "2024-01-01"`
`IN`	Matches any value in a list	`project IN ("WebApp", "API")`
`NOT IN`	Excludes values from a list	`status NOT IN ("Done", "Closed")`
`IS`	Checks for empty values	`resolution IS EMPTY`
`ORDER BY`	Sorts query results	`priority = High ORDER BY created DESC`

4. Combining JQL Clauses with Boolean Operators

Boolean Operator	Description	Example Query
`AND`	Matches both conditions	`status = "In Progress" AND assignee = "jane.doe"`
`OR`	Matches at least one condition	`priority = High OR priority = Medium`
`NOT`	Excludes conditions	`labels NOT IN ("backend")`

Example:

```
project = "WebApp" AND type = Bug AND status NOT IN ("Done", "Closed")
```

📌 This query **finds all open bugs in the "WebApp" project.**

---

5. Searching with Date Functions

JQL allows filtering issues by **dates and time periods.**

Function	Description	Example Query
created	Filters by creation date	created >= "2024-01-01"
updated	Filters by last updated date	updated > "-7d" (Last 7 days)
due	Filters by due date	due < "2024-06-30"
resolved	Filters by resolution date	resolved >= "2024-03-01"

Relative Date Queries:

- created >= -30d → Issues created in the **last 30 days.**
- updated < -7d → Issues **not updated in the last 7 days.**
- duedate = startOfWeek() → Issues **due this week.**

---

6. Advanced JQL Queries for Agile Teams

6.1. Find Issues in the Current Sprint

```
project = "MobileApp" AND sprint IN openSprints()
```

📌 Retrieves **all issues in the active sprint.**

6.2. Find Unassigned High-Priority Bugs

```
project = "API" AND type = Bug AND priority = High AND assignee IS EMPTY
```

📌 **Lists all high-priority bugs that haven't been assigned.**

6.3. Identify Overdue Tasks

```
project = "Backend" AND type = Task AND duedate < now() AND status != "Done"
```

📌 **Finds tasks that are past their due date and not yet completed.**

6.4. Find Issues Assigned to a Specific Team Member

```
assignee = "john.doe" AND status IN ("In Progress", "Review")
```

📌 Lists all open tasks assigned to John Doe.

6.5. Find Issues Resolved Last Week

```
status = "Done" AND resolved >= startOfWeek(-1) AND resolved <= endOfWeek(-1)
```

📌 Finds issues resolved in the previous week.

6.6. Find Epics with No Linked Stories

```
issuetype = Epic AND NOT issueFunction in hasSubtasks()
```

📌 Lists all Epics that do not have child stories linked to them.

7. Using JQL with Jira Dashboards

JQL can be used in **Jira Dashboards and Filters** to create:

■ Custom reports on sprint progress.
📌 Kanban board filters for specific issue types.
🚀 Automated alerts for overdue tasks.

Example Dashboard JQL Queries

Dashboard Widget	JQL Query Example
Sprint Burndown Chart	`sprint IN openSprints() AND status != "Done"`
High-Priority Open Bugs	`project = "WebApp" AND type = Bug AND priority = High AND status != "Done"`
Tasks Due This Week	`duedate >= startOfWeek() AND duedate <= endOfWeek()`
Blocked Issues	`status = Blocked`

8. Tips for Writing Better JQL Queries

■ **Use Filters and Save Queries** → Save frequently used queries for quick access.
■ **Use ORDER BY for Sorted Results** → `ORDER BY updated DESC` shows recent updates first.

■ **Combine Multiple Criteria** → Use AND, OR for more precise filtering.
■ **Avoid Large Queries** → Use LIMIT if supported to prevent performance issues.

Conclusion

JQL is a **powerful tool** that enables developers, project managers, and QA teams to **track issues, manage sprints, and automate reporting** in Jira.

By mastering **basic, intermediate, and advanced JQL queries**, teams can:

✔ **Quickly find relevant issues**.
✔ **Improve backlog management**.
✔ **Enhance reporting with custom dashboards**.
✔ **Streamline Agile workflows with automated filters**.

🚀 **Next Steps:** Start experimenting with JQL in **Jira Advanced Search** and create custom queries that fit your team's needs!

Appendix B: Keyboard Shortcuts for Power Users

Jira **keyboard shortcuts** allow developers and Agile teams to navigate, manage issues, and execute actions faster—without reaching for the mouse.

This cheat sheet includes:
■ **Essential navigation shortcuts** for quick movement.
■ **Issue management shortcuts** for faster edits.
■ **Board navigation shortcuts** for Scrum/Kanban users.
■ **Search and filtering shortcuts** to speed up issue tracking.

🚀 **Master these shortcuts to enhance your efficiency in Jira!**

1. Essential Navigation Shortcuts

Use these shortcuts to **quickly move between Jira views**:

Shortcut	Action
g + d	Go to **Dashboard**
g + p	Go to **Project Page**
g + b	Go to **Boards** (Scrum/Kanban)
g + i	Open **Issues & Filters**
g + a	Open **Administration Panel** (Admin only)
g + l	Open **Jira Labels** page
?	Show **all Jira keyboard shortcuts**

• **Tip:** Use g + [key] to quickly switch between Jira sections.

2. Issue Management Shortcuts

📌 **Quickly create, edit, and transition issues** using these shortcuts:

Shortcut	Action
c	Create a new issue
.	Open the **command palette** (type actions quickly)
e	Edit the selected issue
a	Assign an issue to a user
i	Assign an issue to yourself

m	Add a comment to an issue
l	Add or edit labels
s	Share the issue with a user
w	Watch/unwatch an issue
o	Open the issue in a new tab
z	Toggle full-screen mode

* **Tip:** Use . (dot key) to quickly access issue actions like "Edit," "Assign," or "Close Issue".

3. Issue Transition Shortcuts

📌 **Move issues between workflow statuses with ease**:

Shortcut	Action
t	Transition an issue (Move to next status)
1	Move to **To Do**
2	Move to **In Progress**
3	Move to **In Review**
4	Move to **Done**

* **Tip:** These shortcuts work in **Scrum/Kanban boards and issue views**.

4. Agile Board Navigation Shortcuts

📌 **Quickly move across Scrum or Kanban boards**:

Shortcut	Action
n	Move to the next issue in the backlog
p	Move to the previous issue in the backlog
s	Open issue details in sidebar
t	Transition an issue to the next status
f	Find issues (search in backlog)
j	Move down (next issue)

k	Move up (previous issue)
v	Toggle card view modes
x	Select/deselect an issue

• **Tip:** Use j and k to **scroll through issues quickly** in Scrum/Kanban boards.

---

5. Searching & Filtering Shortcuts

📌 **Speed up searching and filtering issues**:

Shortcut	Action
/	Jump to Quick Search
f	Open the Search Filter panel
u	Open Advanced Search (JQL)
[	Go back in navigation
]	Go forward in navigation

• **Tip:** Use **JQL (Jira Query Language)** for **powerful issue filtering** (see **Appendix A** for a JQL cheat sheet).

---

6. Jira Admin Shortcuts (For Administrators)

📌 **Quick access for Jira Admin users**:

Shortcut	Action
g + a	Open Jira Administration
g + g	Open Global Configuration
g + f	Open Field Configuration
g + s	Open System Settings

• **Tip:** Admin users should **bookmark these shortcuts** for faster Jira setup and configuration.

---

7. Bonus: Shortcut for Command Palette

- ◆ **Press . (dot key)** anytime to **open the command palette**.
- ✔ Type **any action** (e.g., "Create Issue," "Assign Issue," "Close Sprint").
- ✔ Works in **issue view, backlog, boards, and admin panels**.

🚀 **This is the fastest way to perform actions in Jira!**

8. How to Enable Keyboard Shortcuts

- ◆ Keyboard shortcuts are **enabled by default** in Jira Cloud and Jira Data Center.
- ◆ If shortcuts **aren't working**, check:

  - ● Click your profile icon → Personal Settings → Enable **Keyboard Shortcuts**.

9. Printable Jira Shortcuts Quick Reference

📌 **Quick Jira Keyboard Shortcuts for Developers**

Action	Shortcut
Open Quick Search	/
Create a new issue	c
Edit issue	e
Assign issue	a
Assign issue to yourself	i
Add a comment	m
Transition issue	t
Move issue to "To Do"	1
Move issue to "In Progress"	2
Move issue to "Done"	4
Navigate to Dashboard	g + d
Navigate to Issues	g + i
Navigate to Boards	g + b
Show all shortcuts	?

10. Conclusion

Mastering **Jira keyboard shortcuts** can:

✔ **Save time** by reducing mouse clicks.

✔ **Improve workflow speed** in issue management.

✔ **Enhance productivity** when working in Agile/Scrum environments.

🚀 **Next Steps:**

✔ Start **using shortcuts today** in your Jira projects!

✔ Print out this **Jira Shortcut Cheat Sheet** for quick reference.

✔ Experiment with **dot (.) and slash (/) shortcuts** for fast navigation.

By **integrating these shortcuts** into your daily workflow, you'll become a **Jira power user in no time!** ⬤

Appendix C: Glossary of Jira Terms for Developers

Jira comes with a **rich ecosystem of terms** that are essential for developers, product managers, and Agile teams. Understanding these terms will help you **navigate Jira efficiently** and use it to its full potential.

This glossary provides **clear definitions of key Jira terms**, categorized for **quick reference**.

1. General Jira Terms

Term	Definition
Jira	A project management and issue-tracking tool developed by Atlassian, widely used for Agile software development.
Project	A collection of issues grouped together within Jira, representing a software product, feature set, or team workload.
Issue	The fundamental unit in Jira, representing a task, bug, feature request, or improvement.
Workflow	A defined sequence of steps (statuses and transitions) that an issue follows from creation to resolution.
Sprint	A time-boxed development cycle in Scrum methodology, usually lasting 1-4 weeks.
Epic	A high-level feature or large user story that is broken down into smaller stories or tasks.
Story	A user requirement or feature request that contributes to an Epic.
Task	A standard work item in Jira, usually smaller than a Story but larger than a Sub-task.
Sub-task	A smaller work item within a Task or Story that helps break down complex work.
Backlog	A prioritized list of work items (issues) that need to be completed, typically used in Agile projects.
Component	A sub-section within a project that helps categorize and organize issues.
Label	A tag that can be added to issues to enable filtering and classification.
Resolution	The outcome of an issue, defining how it was closed (e.g., "Fixed," "Won't Do," "Duplicate").

2. Jira Issue Types

Issue Type	Definition
Bug	An issue that represents a defect in the software.
Story	A feature request or user requirement in Agile development.
Task	A unit of work that needs to be completed.
Sub-task	A smaller unit of work within a Task or Story.
Epic	A large body of work that can be broken down into smaller Stories and Tasks.

3. Jira Workflow and Statuses

Term	Definition
Status	Represents the current state of an issue (e.g., "To Do," "In Progress," "Done").
Transition	The movement of an issue from one status to another.
Workflow	The sequence of statuses and transitions that an issue follows from creation to resolution.
Custom Workflow	A user-defined workflow that modifies the default Jira workflow to fit specific team needs.
Resolution	The final outcome of an issue, such as "Fixed," "Duplicate," or "Won't Fix."

4. Jira Agile Boards

Term	Definition
Scrum Board	A Jira board used in Scrum methodology to manage Sprints, Backlogs, and Story progress.
Kanban Board	A Jira board used in Kanban methodology to visualize work-in-progress with a continuous workflow.
Swimlanes	Horizontal lanes in a board that group issues based on conditions such as assignee, priority, or Epic.
Columns	Represent different workflow stages (e.g., "To Do," "In Progress," "Review," "Done").

| WIP Limit | A constraint that limits the number of tasks allowed in a particular workflow stage. |
| Work Log | A record of time spent working on an issue. |

5. Jira Fields and Customization

Term	Definition
Custom Field	A user-defined field added to Jira issues for extra information.
Screen	A layout that controls how fields appear when creating, editing, or viewing issues.
Field Configuration	A Jira setting that controls which fields are required, optional, or hidden.
Issue Type Scheme	A configuration that defines which issue types are available for a project.
Permission Scheme	Defines user access levels and actions allowed in a project.

6. Jira Query Language (JQL)

Term	Definition
JQL (Jira Query Language)	A structured query language used to search and filter issues in Jira.
Filter	A saved JQL query that helps users retrieve specific issues.
Smart Query	A JQL feature that suggests searches based on commonly used filters.
Saved Search	A query stored for repeated use, often used in dashboards.

* **Example JQL Query:**

```
project = "MobileApp" AND status = "In Progress"
```

📌 **Finds all issues in the "MobileApp" project that are currently in progress**.

7. Jira Permissions & User Roles

Term	Definition

Administrator	A user with full access to manage Jira settings, workflows, and user permissions.
Project Lead	A user responsible for managing a specific Jira project.
Developer	A team member who works on issues and updates statuses.
Reporter	The user who creates an issue in Jira.
Watcher	A user who follows an issue to receive updates.

8. Jira Integrations & DevOps

Term	Definition
CI/CD (Continuous Integration/Continuous Deployment)	A software practice where code changes are automatically built, tested, and deployed.
Jenkins Integration	Connects Jira with Jenkins to track builds and deployments.
GitHub/GitLab/Bitbucket Integration	Links Jira issues with repositories, pull requests, and commits.
Webhooks	Automation triggers that send updates when specific Jira events occur.
REST API	Jira's API that allows developers to create custom integrations with external tools.

9. Common Jira Reports & Metrics

Report Type	Definition
Burndown Chart	A graph showing work completed vs. remaining work in a sprint.
Velocity Chart	Tracks the amount of work completed across sprints.
Cumulative Flow Diagram (CFD)	Displays the number of issues in each workflow state over time.
Sprint Report	A summary of completed and incomplete work during a sprint.
Cycle Time Report	Measures the time taken for an issue to move from creation to resolution.

10. Miscellaneous Jira Terms

Term	Definition
Confluence	A collaboration tool by Atlassian, often integrated with Jira for documentation.
Trello	A lightweight task management tool, also owned by Atlassian, with Jira integration.
Marketplace Apps	Third-party Jira plugins/extensions that enhance functionality.
Automation Rules	Predefined actions triggered when specific conditions are met in Jira.
SLA (Service Level Agreement)	A time-based goal for resolving issues, often used in Jira Service Management.

Conclusion

Understanding Jira's terminology is essential for **developers, project managers, and Agile teams**. This glossary provides a **quick reference guide** to help you navigate Jira's interface, workflows, and reporting tools more effectively.

🚀 **Next Steps:**
✔ Bookmark this **Jira Glossary** for quick reference.
✔ Explore **JQL queries** to improve search efficiency (See **Appendix A**).
✔ Use **Jira Reports** to track project performance and team productivity.

By mastering these Jira terms, you'll **streamline your development workflow and optimize project tracking!** ●

Appendix D: Resources and Tools for Further Learning

Jira is a **powerful tool for Agile development**, and continuous learning is essential to **mastering its features**. This appendix provides **recommended resources** to deepen your Jira expertise, improve Agile workflows, and integrate Jira with other DevOps tools.

Below, you'll find:
■ **Official Jira documentation & training**
■ **Jira-related books & courses**
■ **Communities & forums**
■ **Jira marketplace apps & integrations**
■ **Useful blogs & YouTube channels**

🚀 **Use this guide to become a Jira expert!**

1. Official Atlassian Resources

📌 **These are the best places to start if you want to learn Jira directly from Atlassian**:

Resource	Description	Link
Jira Software Documentation	Official Atlassian guide covering Jira setup, features, and troubleshooting.	[Jira Docs] (https://support.atlassian.com/jira-software/)
Atlassian University	Paid & free training courses on Jira, Agile, and DevOps.	[Atlassian University] (https://university.atlassian.com/)
Jira Community Forum	Ask questions, share tips, and connect with Jira users worldwide.	[Atlassian Community] (https://community.atlassian.com/)
Jira Software Blog	Updates, best practices, and feature announcements from Atlassian.	[Atlassian Blog] (https://www.atlassian.com/blog)
Jira Cloud API Docs	Reference for integrating Jira with external tools using the REST API.	[Jira API Docs] (https://developer.atlassian.com/cloud/jira/platform/rest/v3/)

♦ **Tip:** Bookmark these links to quickly find help when working with Jira.

2. Books on Jira and Agile Project Management

📌 **Expand your Jira knowledge with books written by industry experts**:

Book Title	Author	Description

Jira Software Essentials	Patrick Li	Covers Jira fundamentals, issue tracking, and Agile workflows.
Practical Jira Administration	Matthew Doar	A hands-on guide for Jira administrators and power users.
The Art of Agile Development	James Shore	Covers Agile principles and how to implement them in Jira.
Scrum: The Art of Doing Twice the Work in Half the Time	Jeff Sutherland	A foundational book on Scrum methodology used in Jira.

- **Tip:** If you're new to Agile, start with *Scrum: The Art of Doing Twice the Work in Half the Time.*

3. Online Courses & Certifications

📌 **Take your Jira skills to the next level with these online courses**:

Platform	Course Name	Link
Udemy	Jira for Beginners: Learn Jira Step by Step	[Udemy Jira Course] (https://www.udemy.com/courses/search/?q=jira)
Coursera	Agile with Jira	[Coursera Jira Course] (https://www.coursera.org/learn/jira-agile)
LinkedIn Learning	Learning Jira Software	[LinkedIn Jira Course] (https://www.linkedin.com/learning/learning-jira-software)
Pluralsight	Mastering Jira Software	[Pluralsight Jira Course] (https://www.pluralsight.com/)
Atlassian University	Jira Software Essentials	[Atlassian University] (https://university.atlassian.com/)

- **Tip:** Udemy often has **discounted courses**—check for promotions before purchasing!

4. Communities & Discussion Forums

📌 **Join these communities to stay up-to-date and solve problems faster**:

Community	Description	Link
Atlassian Community	Official forum where Jira users & experts discuss features and solutions.	[Atlassian Community] (https://community.atlassian.com/)

r/jira (Reddit)	Subreddit for Jira-related discussions and troubleshooting.	[Reddit Jira] (https://www.reddit.com/r/jira/)
Stack Overflow	Find answers to Jira API & development-related queries.	[Stack Overflow] (https://stackoverflow.com/questions/tagged/jira)
LinkedIn Jira Groups	Professional groups for sharing Jira best practices.	[LinkedIn Jira Groups] (https://www.linkedin.com/)

* **Tip:** The **Atlassian Community** is the best place to **get fast answers** from Jira experts.

5. Jira Marketplace Apps & Integrations

📌 **Enhance Jira's functionality with these top-rated apps**:

App Name	Purpose	Link
ScriptRunner	Advanced automation & scripting in Jira.	[ScriptRunner] (https://marketplace.atlassian.com/apps/6820/scriptrunner-for-jira)
Zephyr	Test management integration for Jira.	[Zephyr] (https://marketplace.atlassian.com/apps/1014684/zephyr-scale)
BigPicture	Agile roadmaps & project portfolio management.	[BigPicture] (https://marketplace.atlassian.com/apps/1216237/bigpicture)
Xray	Advanced test management for Agile teams.	[Xray] (https://marketplace.atlassian.com/apps/1211769/xray-test-management)
Jira Misc Workflow Extensions (JMWE)	Adds powerful workflow automation features.	[JMWE] (https://marketplace.atlassian.com/apps/292/jira-misc-workflow-extensions)

* **Tip:** If you're a developer, **ScriptRunner** is a must-have for automating Jira workflows.

6. Blogs & YouTube Channels

📌 **Follow these blogs and YouTube channels for Jira tutorials, tips, and updates**:

Resource	Type	Link

Atlassian Blog	Blog	[Atlassian Blog] (https://www.atlassian.com/blog)
Ricksoft Blog	Blog	[Ricksoft Jira Tips] (https://www.ricksoft-inc.com/)
Jira Guru (YouTube)	YouTube Channel	[Jira Guru YouTube] (https://www.youtube.com/c/Jira Guru)
Atlassian YouTube	YouTube Channel	[Atlassian YouTube] (https://www.youtube.com/user/G oAtlassian)
Dan Talks Tech (YouTube)	YouTube Channel	[Dan Talks Tech] (https://www.youtube.com/c/Dan TalksTech)

- **Tip:** Subscribe to the **Atlassian YouTube Channel** for official Jira updates and tutorials.

7. DevOps & Agile Learning Resources

📌 **If you want to go beyond Jira and learn about DevOps & Agile, check these out**:

Resource	Description	Link
Scrum Guide	The official Scrum methodology guide.	[Scrum Guide] (https://scrumguides.org/)
DevOps Handbook	A must-read book on DevOps best practices.	[DevOps Handbook] (https://itrevolution.com/book/the-devops-handbook/)
Agile Manifesto	The core principles of Agile development.	[Agile Manifesto] (https://agilemanifesto.org/)

- **Tip:** Bookmark the **Scrum Guide** if you're working in Agile environments.

Conclusion

With Jira's vast ecosystem, **ongoing learning is key** to becoming a **power user**. Use these resources to:
✔ **Deepen your Jira knowledge**
✔ **Improve Agile workflows**
✔ **Automate and integrate Jira with DevOps tools**

🚀 **Next Steps:**

- Bookmark this **Resources & Tools guide** for quick reference.
- Subscribe to **Jira blogs & YouTube channels** for regular updates.
- Take a **Jira course** to strengthen your skills.

By leveraging these resources, you'll **stay ahead in Agile software development and Jira mastery!** ●

Conclusion

Jira has become an indispensable tool for **developers, Agile teams, and software organizations** looking to streamline their development processes. Throughout this book, we have explored how Jira can be **configured, optimized, and integrated** to support high-efficiency software development cycles.

By now, you should have a **deep understanding of Jira**, from setting up projects and workflows to **automating repetitive tasks, managing dependencies, and integrating with CI/CD pipelines**. Whether you're a developer working within an Agile team, a technical lead overseeing multiple projects, or an administrator fine-tuning Jira for efficiency, you now have the knowledge and best practices to make Jira work for you.

🚀 Key Takeaways

1 **Jira is a powerful tool for software teams** – It provides end-to-end visibility into projects, making Agile development more structured and manageable.

2 **Customization is key** – Jira's flexibility allows you to tailor workflows, issue types, boards, and automation to fit your team's needs.

3 **Integration enhances efficiency** – By connecting Jira to your IDE, Git repository, CI/CD pipeline, and DevOps tools, you can **streamline your development workflow**.

4 **Automation saves time** – Jira Automation can reduce manual work, enforce consistency, and **enhance productivity across teams**.

5 **Scaling and optimizing Jira is crucial** – As your development team grows, refining permissions, project structures, and performance optimizations ensures a **smooth experience**.

6 **Jira will continue to evolve** – Keeping up with **cloud-first trends and AI-driven automation** will help you future-proof your setup.

⬛ What's Next?

Mastering Jira is an ongoing journey. Here's how you can continue improving:

✔ **Experiment with advanced Jira features** – Try new automation rules, JQL queries, or custom scripts to further optimize workflows.

✔ **Stay engaged with the Jira community** – Join **Atlassian forums, LinkedIn groups, and Jira meetups** to exchange best practices and learn from experts.

✔ **Explore new integrations** – Investigate marketplace apps like **ScriptRunner, Zephyr, and BigPicture** to enhance Jira's capabilities.

✔ **Keep learning** – Follow **Atlassian University, online courses, and tech blogs** to stay updated with Jira's latest features and industry trends.

✔ **Apply Agile best practices** – The most effective Jira users **align their workflow with Agile principles** to ensure efficient sprint planning, backlog grooming, and software delivery.

🔔 Final Thoughts

Jira is **more than just a task tracker**—it's a **strategic development tool** that can transform how software teams work together. By leveraging its features effectively, you can **reduce friction in project management, improve team collaboration, and deliver high-quality software faster**.

Whether you are just starting with Jira or refining your existing setup, the insights from this book will help you **maximize Jira's potential and build a streamlined, high-efficiency development cycle**.

Thank you for taking this journey through **Jira for Developers: Streamlining Your Development Projects**. Wishing you success in your projects, and may your Jira workflows always stay **efficient, optimized, and developer-friendly!**

🚀 **Happy coding and Agile planning!**